The
Web Wizard's
Guide to

Web Design

THE WEB WIZARD'S GUIDE TO WEB DESIGN

JAMES G. LENGEL

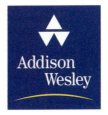

Boston San Francisco New York
London Toronto Sydney Tokyo Singapore Madrid
Mexico City Munich Paris Cape Town Hong Kong Montreal

Executive Editor: *Susan Hartman Sullivan*
Associate Editor: *Elinor Actipis*
Executive Marketing Manager: *Michael Hirsch*
Managing Editor: *Pat Mahtani*
Production Supervision: *Diane Freed*
Cover and Interior Designer: *Leslie Haimes*
Design Manager: *Regina Hagen*
Composition: *Gillian Hall, The Aardvark Group*
Copyeditor: *Betsy Hardinger*
Proofreader: *Holly McLean-Aldis*
Manufacturing Coordinator: *Caroline Fell*

Access the latest information about Addison-Wesley titles from our World Wide Web site: *http://www.aw.com/cs*

Many of the designations used by manufacturers and sellers to distinguish their products are claimed as trademarks. Where those designations appear in this book, and Addison-Wesley was aware of a trademark claim, the designations have been printed in initial caps or all caps.

The programs and the applications presented in this book have been included for their instructional value. They have been tested with care but are not guaranteed for any particular purpose. The publisher does not offer any warranties or representations, nor does it accept any liabilities with respect to the programs or applications.

Library of Congress Cataloging-in-Publication Data
Lengel, James G.
    The Web wizard's guide to web design / by James G. Lengel.
        p. cm.
    Includes index.
    ISBN 0-201-74562-3 (alk. paper)
        1. Web sites--Design. I. Title.

TK5105.888 .L46 2002
005.7'2--dc21   2001034320

ISBN 0-201-74562-3

1 2 3 4 5 6 7 8 9 10—QWT—04030201

TABLE OF CONTENTS

PREFACE

About Addison-Wesley's Web Wizard Series

The beauty of the Web is that, with a little effort, anyone can harness its power to create sophisticated Web sites. Addison-Wesley's Web Wizard Series helps students master the Web by presenting a concise introduction to one important Internet topic or technology in each book. The books start from square one and assume no prior experience with the technology being covered. Mastering the Web doesn't come with a wave of a magic wand; but by studying these accessible, highly visual textbooks, readers will be well on their way.

The series is written by instructors who are familiar with the challenges beginners face when learning the material. To this end, the Web Wizard books offer more than a cookbook approach: they emphasize principles and offer clear explanations, giving the reader a strong foundation of knowledge on which to build.

Numerous features highlight important points and aid in learning:

⭐ Tips — important points to keep in mind

⭐ Shortcuts — timesaving ideas

⭐ Warnings — things to watch out for

⭐ Do It Yourself — activities to try now

⭐ Review questions and hands-on exercises

⭐ Online references — Web sites to visit to obtain more information

Supplementary materials for the books, including updates, additional examples, and source code, are available at `http://www.aw.com/webwizard`. Also available for qualified instructors adopting a book from the series are instructor's manuals, sample tests, and solutions. Please contact your Addison-Wesley sales representative for the instructor resources password

About This Book

The Web Wizard's Guide to Web Design takes you through the entire process of planning and building a Web site, starting by specifying the needs of your audience, setting forth the structure, designing the display, and gathering the materials — including multimedia. The book goes on to show you how to build the site with a WYSIWYG editor, and then how to test and post the site to a Web server.

If you are a beginner building your first Web site, this book will start you on your way. Yet if you are a professional Web designer, the planning, design, and building techniques that are covered will further enhance your skills. The best way to use this book is to build your own Web site as you go through the chapters. At each step in the process, you will find *Do It Yourself* exercises embedded in the text that encourage you to actually build the site as you learn the basic concepts. The book follows the model of plan, gather, build: First you plan the site, in some detail; then you gather and prepare the contents of the site; and, finally, you build the site.

The methods described in this book are based on my experience teaching hundreds of students in the Computers in Communication course at Boston University over the last seven years how to design and publish their own Web sites. To all of those students at the Boston University College of Communication who built their first Web site in my classroom, I extend a hearty thanks for their inspiration and contributions to this book. I also appreciate the support and leadership of College Dean Brent Baker, which has made possible this course of study. The reviewers of the manuscript, whose suggestions have made he book clearer and more accurate, include John Beatty, La Salle University; George Campbell, george design; Bert H. Hoff, North Seattle Community College; Rebecca Lawson, Lansing Community College; Emily Stern, The College of New Rochelle; and Ray Trygstad, Illinois Institute of Technology.

Thanks go to my family for their support and understanding of the process of writing this book. *The Web Wizard's Guide to Web Design* is dedicated to the memory of my father, Henry E. "Murph" Lengel.

James G. Lengel
June 2001

CHAPTER ONE

PLANNING A WEB SITE

T his chapter explains how to determine the purposes and objectives of your Web site before you build it. You'll learn the key elements of creating the conceptual design: identifying your audience, determining the site's purpose, and planning the site's structure. You'll also get acquainted with the myriad Web tools available for communicating your ideas, including text, images, multimedia, and interactivity.

Chapter Objectives

- Learn how to identify and describe the audience for your Web site
- Understand how to determine and describe your site's purpose
- Learn how to plan and chart your site's structure
- Understand the possibilities of communication through your site
- Complete a planning table to document your site's design

Identifying the Audience for Your Site

Building a Web site is a lot like preparing a meal. When you're planning a meal, you start by deciding what you'll serve, in what order, and to whom. Then you gather the ingredients from the cupboard, the garden, or the supermarket. With all the parts ready, you begin assembling each dish. The dishes you're preparing are like the pages in a Web site. Each dish contains various ingredients, and when the diners are finished with one course, they go on to the next. This book assumes that you are responsible for planning, creating, building, and maintaining a Web site. In our restaurant analogy, you're responsible for planning, gathering the ingredients, cooking each dish, and serving the diners. You may even be called on to clear the plates and clean up afterward.

The most important people in a restaurant are not the cooks, the waiters, or even the owners, but the customers. They're the ones who determine whether it succeeds or fails. Successful cooks know the needs tastes of their diners. They watch them eat, and they seek their reactions to the food. If most of the diners at a restaurant are in a hurry, the cook makes short-order meals. If the restaurant caters to leisurely gourmets, the chef prepares a multicourse meal with all the trimmings. The staff learns to recognize repeat customers and steer them to their favorite table and preferred dishes.

Similarly, successful Web sites serve the needs of their audiences. This means that a Web site designer must know who the audience is, why they came to the site, what they are looking for, and how they think. No matter how efficient a programmer or how deft an artist you are, your site will not succeed unless it serves the needs of its visitors. So the first step is to understand who your audience is.

Three Sites, Three Audiences

Figures 1.1, 1.2, and 1.3 show the home pages of three Web sites. Can you identify the audience for each site?

The audience for Yahooligans is young children who are looking for things on the Internet. For Fidelity, the audience is adult investors who are looking for information and advice. For the National Oceanic and Atmospheric Administration (NOAA), the audience is wider, ranging from meteorologists to research scientists to professional anglers, all of whom are interested in the weather. The design and content of these three sites are completely different because the audiences are different. Each design is built around the needs of its audience.

Children need limited choices, pictorial representations of ideas, and simple words. These needs are evident in the design of the Yahooligans home page and throughout the site. Investors who are visiting the Fidelity site need easy and quick access to many types of information, with a complex and specialized vocabulary. They have little need for pictures. The NOAA has multiple audiences and needs to present all of them with the choices they are looking for. From the beginning, the designers of these three sites considered the nature and interests of their potential visitors.

Figure 1.1 Yahooligans Web Page

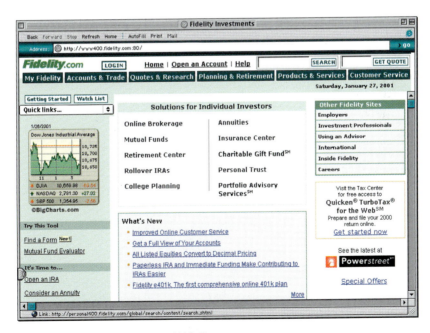

Figure 1.2 Fidelity Investments Web Page

Figure 1.3 NOAA Web Page

Most Web designers work for the site sponsor, either as employees or under contract. It would be easy for a Web designer to plan and build the site around the needs and experiences of the sponsor. But it's important to remember that the sponsor is not the audience. Instead, the audience is the people who use the site to gather information, entertain themselves, or conduct business. In most cases, these users are the customers of the sponsor, and not the sponsor itself.

User-Centered Design

When you're designing a site, you must consider many things. It's natural to think first of the demands of the client organization, but you must also keep in mind the needs of the users. And the possibilities and limitations of computer and Internet technologies must necessarily be brought to bear on the planning process. Which of these three considerations is most important?

Organization-centered Web sites are built from the point of view of the company or group that is publishing the site. These sites are easy to recognize. The site's structure often reflects the sponsor's organizational chart, and the vocabulary reflects the language used by company executives among themselves to describe the organization. The content of the site parallels internal company documents, such as job descriptions and division mission statements. Figure 1.4 shows a hypothetical Web site for a fictional hospital.

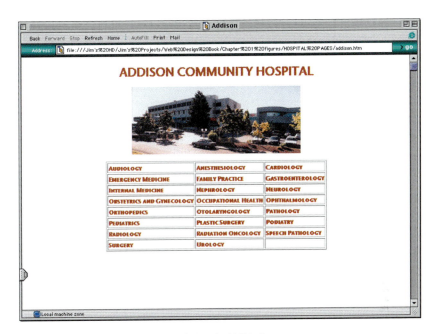

Figure 1.4 Organization-Centered Hospital Web Page

In this example, the structure, content, and vocabulary are familiar to the hospital's employees and managers. They know that radiology is where you find X-rays and that pediatrics deals with children. But would this site work well with the general public, especially those who have little hospital experience or a limited education?

The design of **technology-centered** Web sites starts with a particular set of tools (often, the ones favored by or familiar to the designer), and the site is built around the features of that technology. If the hospital were to contract its Web site development to a designer who has expertise in Macromedia Flash, for instance, the site would probably end up with lots of animation and graphics. Another contractor might build the same site around a database technology, publishing the site using Active Server Pages and including lots of forms to fill out. A contractor with strength and experience in multimedia technologies might include television-like interviews with hospital executives and feature a live video stream from the operating room.

There is nothing wrong with using the latest technologies, but they have the potential of overshadowing the essential purpose of the Web site and the needs and interests of the people who use it.

The design of a **user-centered** Web site begins with the situation of the people who make up the target audience. The designer first defines these visitors, studies them to figure out what they need and how they work, and then presents the client organization in terms that visitors can understand and in a structure that mirrors the way they think. The designer employs whatever technologies are necessary to make the Web site work for its users. Figure 1.5 shows an actual user-centered hospital Web site.

Figure 1.5 User-Centered Hospital Web Page

This site uses the vocabulary of the general public to describe the hospital's services. The site is structured around choices that fit the way the audience thinks about health issues. As a result, it is more effective than organization- or technology-centered sites.

This book teaches you how to design and build user-centered Web sites. That's why it's so important to define your audience as the first step in designing your Web site. If you don't have a clear idea of the needs and interests of the people who will use the site, you run the risk of developing a site that focuses on the wrong things and does not accomplish its objectives.

Ways of Defining Your Audience

The audience for a Web site can be defined in a number of ways:

1. By age
2. By gender
3. By geographic location
4. By residence: urban, suburban, rural

5. By level of income

6. By level of education

7. By race or ethnicity

8. By interest (the reason the user came to the site)

9. By history (the path of Web pages that the user has visited before)

The characteristics in the Categories 1 through 7 are called **demographics**. For many decades, demographics have been used to define audiences for television commercials and newspaper advertisements. In defining the audience for your Web site, you'll find that demographics are relevant but not nearly as important as the final two categories.

The audience for the Yahooligans Web site in Figure 1.1 might be defined as follows:

> *Children between 8 and 12 years old who are looking for information relevant to their school or personal research.*

This definition includes one demographic characteristic (age) as well as one interest characteristic (looking for information). The more characteristics you can include, the more precise and useful your definition will be. Here is an example of a narrowly defined audience:

> *Fidelity brokerage customers living in large cities with balances of at least $250,000 who have conducted at least three online stock trades in the last three weeks and who have clicked on the Trade button on the Fidelity home page.*

This definition includes two demographic characteristics (location and wealth) as well as two characteristics regarding the user's interests and history. The more precisely you define the audience for your site, the easier it is to design a Web site that works.

Steps in Defining Your Audience

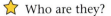 **DO IT YOURSELF**   Define Your Audience

As you work through this book, you should have in mind a Web site that you will be designing. This site might be a course project, a site you are building for a sponsor, or a hypothetical site you might like to build someday. At each step, you will use this site as your example. Here, your first task is to define the audience for the site.

A good way to define your audience is to picture the kind of person who will be accessing the site. Imagine your visitors sitting at their computers engaged with your site. Then ask these questions about them:

⭐ Who are they?

⭐ Why are they at the site?

⭐ How did they get there?

⭐ How old are they? What's the range of their ages?

⭐ Where do they live?

⭐ What gender are they? Mostly men? Women? Why?

⭐ How wealthy are they, compared with the rest of the population?

⭐ What's their history of dealing with your organization? What have they done before at your Web site?

⭐ Are there any common characteristics that stand out?

The answers to these questions can form the basis of your audience definition. Here's an audience definition for a site sponsored by a company that sells products for left-handers:

> *The audience for the LeftyStuff Web site is potential purchasers of LeftyStuff products who have responded to one of LeftyStuff's banner ads and are interested in items designed especially for left-handed people. Most are adults, equally divided among men and women, between 25 and 50 years of age, who live in the United States or Canada, are sports-minded, and have family incomes greater than $50,000. Most have never visited the site before.*

This definition is specific and useful. Creating this kind of audience definition forces you to think through the nature of your audience and to better understand its needs and interests.

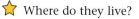 Determining Your Site's Purpose

After you know *who* will be using your site, you must think about *what* they will be using it for, and *why*. Part of the site's purpose comes from users' reasons for visiting the site and so is already evident in the audience definition. The rest of the purpose is based on the organization's reasons for publishing the site. Here is a sample statement of purpose, based on the hypothetical LeftyStuff Web site described in the preceding section.

> *The purpose of the LeftyStuff Web site is to increase the direct online sales of high-end tennis racquets by 30% over the next three quarters. The site will display six key items from the racquet line, with two types of color photos: the racquets alone and the racquets in use by left-handers on the tennis court. The site will make it easy for customers to find racquets that best meet their needs and will make it easy to purchase the racquet online using a credit card. The site will also communicate the mission of the LeftyStuff Corporation and its special emphasis on the needs of this minority group.*

This definition of purpose reflects both the organization's needs (to market and sell racquets) and the customer's interests (to find and purchase a specialty racquet). It explains *why* the site is being published (to increase sales) as well as *what* it will include (product displays, a purchasing system, and the company mission). The key to the definition lies in the verbs that describe the site's functions:

⭐ *Increase* sales

⭐ *Display* items

⭐ *Find* the racquet

⭐ *Purchase* the racquet

⭐ *Communicate* the mission

For each of the Web sites pictured in Figures 1.6 and 1.7, how would you state the purpose?

The purpose of the Web site of *The Financial Times* might be to provide the news and advertising content to online readers along with additional searching, updating, and multimedia features not available in the printed newspaper. The purpose of the J. Crew site might be to increase purchases of J. Crew clothing by displaying selected products with photos and written descriptions, and making it easy for the customer to select items, check availability, order the items, and pay online.

Figure 1.6 Financial Times Web Page

Figure 1.7 J. Crew Web Page

Goals and Objectives

The statement of purpose for your Web site should contain both goals and objectives. **Goals** state the desired long-term results, such as "to increase the direct online sales of high-end tennis racquets by 30% over the next three quarters." Goals are most often organization-centered, but they can be user-centered as well, such as "to provide a wider range of services to online readers of the newspaper."

Objectives include specific means and methods used on the site to accomplish its goals, such as "to provide online readers of the newspaper with hourly updates of key news stories" or "to display six key items from the racquet line, with two types of color photos: the items alone and the racquets in use by left-handers on the tennis court." Objectives are most often stated in user-centered terms.

In planning your site, you need to create both kinds of statements. The goals keep you focused on the larger purposes of the organization, and the objectives set forth specific and measurable features that the site must include. Here is the statement of purpose for an actual Web site:

> *The chief purpose of the XYZ Web site is to expand and broaden the reach of the program so that it makes a greater impact on American education. A secondary purpose is to create a virtual community of educators interested in XYZ, who can use the Internet to share ideas and promote sound teaching in this field in middle and high schools. A tertiary purpose of this site is to serve as a model or template for other XYZ programs that seek to promote change and improvement in education.*

To achieve these broad purposes, the site will comprise three key objectives:

- *To inform its audiences about XYZ happenings*
- *To educate its audiences about XYZ*
- *To promote intelligent conversation about XYZ among all three audiences*

From this statement of purpose, can you pick out which are goals, and which objectives?

Organization and User Purposes

In the statement just discussed, can you also pick out which goals and objectives are user-centered, and which are organization-centered? A user-centered objective might be "to promote intelligent conversation about XYZ among all three audiences." An organization-centered goal might be "to expand and broaden the reach of the program so that it makes a greater impact on American education." A good statement of a Web site's purpose will include both user-centered and organization-centered goals and objectives.

Some Web sites also include technology-centered statements of purpose, such as "to show the capabilities of ABC-VR software by including four virtual reality panoramas on the site" or "to allow users to view video excerpts from the summer institutes in a variety of formats, including QuickTime and RealVideo." Most Web sites serve a variety of purposes, and during the planning stage it's important to consider and include all of them.

Evaluating Success

How will you know whether your Web site is a success? How will you measure its effectiveness? After the site has been published and people have used it for a while, you certainly should evaluate it based on the purposes that you developed in the planning stage. You will list each purpose and determine whether it has been accomplished.

Did the sales of left-handed tennis racquets grow by 30%? How many new readers registered at the *Financial Times* online? How many virtual reality panoramas were included in the site? How much intelligent conversation took place among members on the site? The answers to these questions will determine whether the Web site has succeeded in its mission. So it's important that the purposes of the site be described completely and carefully at this early planning stage.

Stating Your Site's Purpose

⭐ **DO IT YOURSELF   State the Purpose**

What is the purpose of your Web site? Include both broad goals and specific objectives. Speak to the goals of the sponsor as well as the needs of the individual users. Include enough detail to assist in planning the site's structure and in evaluating its success. Set goals and objectives for what will be displayed and what users will be able to do in terms of interactivity and communication. Include any specific technologies to be used.

Use the form shown in Figure 1.8 to help you develop your statement of purpose.

Goals of the organization	
Goals of the user	
Objectives for display	
Objectives for interactivity	
Objectives for communication	
Objectives for technology	

Figure 1.8 Template for Statement of Purpose

You'll use this statement of purpose in developing the structure of the site.

Planning the Structure of the Site

Now that you know the site's audience and purposes, you are ready to set forth its **structure**: the layout and functions of each of its parts. The structure typically consists of a diagrammatic flow chart and a detailed written statement of functions. Figure 1.9 shows a sample flow chart.

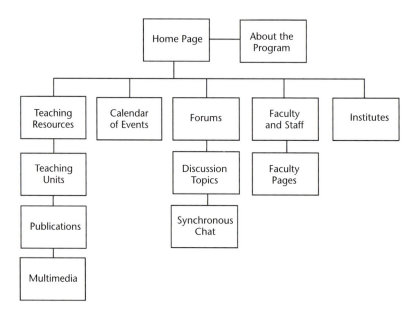

Figure 1.9 Sample Structure Flow Chart

The site illustrated in this chart has a home page and five main sections. Each of the sections serves a unique purpose and provides its own functionality. The Teaching Resources section lets users search a database of lesson plans and video clips. The Calendar of Events section displays information for site visitors day by day and week by week. The Forums section allows visitors to interact with other visitors. The Faculty and Staff section displays photos as well as text biographical sketches of the teachers. In the Institutes section, users can learn what happens at the summer institute and sign up for it online.

No two Web sites have the same structure because each structure is designed to serve the needs of the audience and the purpose of the site. To get acquainted with a different structure, go to a site that you use often. Browse through it to get an idea of its structure. Then draw a diagram of its basic sections, like the flow chart in Figure 1.9. How is this site's structure different from the illustration?

A flow chart is a useful tool for structuring a Web site, but it needs the additional detail provided by a statement of functions. Here is a description of one of the sections of the Web site in Figure 1.9:

Teaching Resources section

This is the largest part of the site, containing materials to help teachers integrate media and democracy topics into the curriculum. It contains three subsections:

- *Teaching units: developed at the summer institutes and contributed to the site by its users, indexed and available in full text online*

- *Publications: references to print and on-line publications and studies, listed and summarized by program faculty and staff, with links to purchasing them online*

- *Multimedia: Video, audio, image, and slide material collected by program staff from institutes and other sources*

All of these are searchable by topic, grade level, and other relevant criteria.

The preceding statements describe *what* is in the Web site. The structure plan must also explain *how* some of the key functions of the site will work. Here's an example:

Functions

In addition to the functions typically available in a Web site, the XYZ site will require additional functionality to implement the materials described above. These include the following:

- *Dynamic home page: Program staff need the capability to change the images and text on the home page at least weekly, without reprogramming the page.*

- *Database of resources: Viewers need to be able to search and retrieve teaching units from a collection of several hundred. Program staff need to be able to add new units to this database easily and index them appropriately.*

- *Database of publications and studies: Viewers need to be able to search and retrieve summaries of relevant publications from a collection of several dozen. Program staff need to be able to add new units to this database easily and index them appropriately.*

- *Streaming video: Excerpts from summer institutes and other multimedia material need to be made available to users in streaming format.*

Describing the Site's Functions

To design the site's structure, it's best to begin with a written description of its functions. These functions should flow directly from the site's statement of purpose. For example, suppose one of the objectives of a Web site is "to promote intelligent *conversation* about XYZ among teachers and media experts." This means that one of the elements of the site's structure should be "to include a discussion board to which users can post questions and comments for perusal by other users."

A good way to develop the site's structure is to list the goals and objectives you specified earlier. Then, for each one, write a statement of functionality. Table 1.1 shows an example.

Table 1.1 Site Structure Template

Purpose	Structure
To *inform* its audiences about XYZ happenings	Calendar of Events section: Here viewers will find a listing of various types of events: *workshops and institutes*, offered by the program by others; *media events* judged by program staff to be especially useful for teaching, with a special emphasis on online events; and *online discussions and chats* offered by the program. Viewers can search events by topic, date, and other criteria.
To *educate* its audiences about XYZ	Institutes section: This section will display publicity and registration information for summer institutes and other workshops offered by the program and its affiliates. Links to teaching resources and video clips will help to show the nature of the institutes, and an online application form will facilitate registration.
To promote intelligent *conversation* about XYZ among all three audiences	Forums section: This section will include the asynchronous discussion system as well as the synchronous chat functions. Viewers will go here to read about new ideas, follow the thread of a topic they are interested in, and compose and post their own two cents' worth. At first, a limited number of topics, perhaps half a dozen, will be posted by program staff; as the use of the site grows, more topics will be added.

The more concrete and detailed the description of the functions, the easier it will be to build the site. Typically, the functionality is described in terms of actions taken by users, such as "Viewers go here to read about new ideas" or "Viewers find many different types of events." Describing the structure from the user's perspective will help you keep the site user-centered.

★DO IT YOURSELF   **Describe the Structure**

Using the style of the examples shown here, describe the structure and functions of your Web site in writing. Create a table, copy your site's objectives into the left column, and then describe your structures and functions in the right column.

Drawing a Flow Chart

When you draw your Web site as a flow chart, the site seems to come to life. You can see the structure and the users' path through the information. A flow chart is a kind of graphical shorthand that represents the site's detailed verbal description. A flow chart can start simply, with a row of blocks (rectangles), each one representing a section of the site. As you develop the structure, the chart becomes more detailed until each block represents a single page in the site. Figure 1.10 shows a portion of the flow chart for the education site introduced earlier.

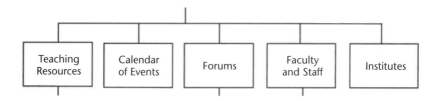

Figure 1.10 A Portion of a Flow Chart

Each of the five sections of the site is represented by a block. The Teaching Resources section, for instance, will contain links to hundreds of Web pages, but at this level of the flow chart it's represented by one block. As you develop the flow chart, you'll add blocks to represent separate functions and, later, separate pages. The next level down in one of the blocks might look like Figure 1.11.

Each of the functions that supports this section—setting search criteria, listing the titles of the resources, and displaying the results—takes up one block at this level. At the next and most detailed level, these functions are spelled out in terms of individual Web pages that the user sees, as shown in Figure 1.12.

Each block now represents one Web page. The site will contain a page for selecting search criteria, another page for displaying the results of the search, and another set of pages for displaying each resource that's found. This last set may include hundreds of pages, which are represented in the flow chart as a continuing series of identically styled pages.

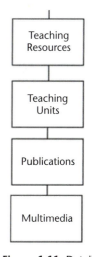

Figure 1.11 Detail from a Flow Chart

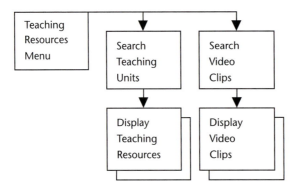

Figure 1.12 Detailed Flow Chart

Speccing Out the Flow Chart

You can make your flow chart more useful if you use it to specify certain important characteristics of the pages you've blocked out. *Speccing out* is a slang expression derived from the verb *specify*. When you spec out a Web page, you list all the items that it will include. You list its filename, its graphics, its text, its menu items, its multimedia elements, and its input forms. Figure 1.13 shows an example.

Figure 1.13 Specced Out Page from Flow Chart

Armed with this information, the Web site builder will find it easy to develop this page. At this point, you don't concern yourself with the visual design or color or "look and feel" of the Web site. Instead, you focus your planning on the functions that the site will perform for the user. These are the essence of a Web site.

An adage from architecture and industrial design is appropriate here: *Form follows function*. Design the functions first, describing them from the user's perspective. Then create the form (what I've called the structure) of the site to fulfill these functions. Colors, designs, logos, and technologies are all forms that must come later, subservient to the functional needs of the user.

Draw Your Flow Chart

> **DO IT YOURSELF** **Draw a Flow Chart**
>
> Now it's time to draw a flow chart for your site. Begin with the basic sections, and then specify the blocks until you have at least some sections completely specced out.

You can draw your flow chart using pencil and paper, or you can use a word processor such as Microsoft Word, which has built-in tools for this purpose. To access these tools, click **Toolbars** from Word's View menu, and then click **Drawing**. The Drawing toolbar shown in Figure 1.14 will open.

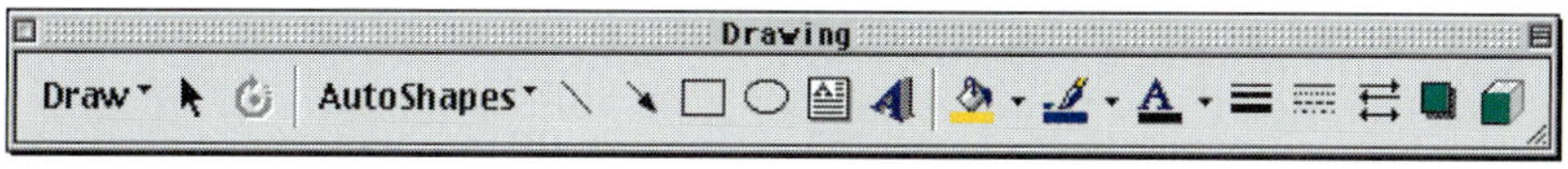

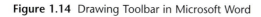

Figure 1.14 Drawing Toolbar in Microsoft Word

To create a block, you use the rectangle tool. You can also create blocks as text boxes by clicking **Text Box** in Word's Insert menu. To create arrows to indicate the links between sections or pages, use the line tool or the arrow tool in the Drawing toolbar.

> **SHORTCUT** **Use Copy and Paste**
>
> It can be time-consuming to create block after identical block in your flow chart. To save time, you can copy and paste blocks to produce multiple blocks of identical size.

For a complex Web site, you may want to create the basic, high-level flow chart on a single sheet of paper. Then create a new, more detailed flow chart for each section of the site, and on these sheets spec out the details described in the preceding section. The ultimate level of detail for each page includes the following:

- The page's filename
- A brief description of the text
- Descriptions of the images
- Descriptions of each sound, video, or animation
- A list of any input forms
- A list of links to other pages

As you can see, this stage of planning can be complex and time-consuming, and it often forces you to think through key aspects of the project. That's why it is important. The flow chart and written specifications that you're developing will form the basis of the design, content, programming, and production of the site.

If building a Web site is like preparing and serving a meal, then the work you've done so far amounts to writing the recipe. You haven't yet gone to the market, lit the oven, or cracked an egg. But you've come a long way toward pleasing your guests by planning a repast that's built around their needs and tastes.

◎◎ Understanding the Possibilities of the Web

A good cook visits many restaurants and eats many meals. Before attempting to work magic in the kitchen, the cook spends a great deal of time in the dining room to better understand what a good meal looks and tastes like. As you plan your Web site, you should do the same thing. To understand the many possibilities for communicating over the Internet, you should visit a variety of Web sites. Look for sites published by various organizations, serving various purposes, reaching diverse audiences, and using a range of technologies.

Understanding the possibilities of the Web will help you to select the best Web site functions and structures to serve your site's purposes. A personal computer connected to the Internet can be used to communicate with your audience in many ways, including the one-way communication you see in the traditional media as well as new forms of interactive and two-way communication. The Web lets you take advantage of most of the ways that human beings have invented to communicate: the human voice; images; text; sound and music; animation; motion video; and virtual reality. All these are among the possibilities you have to choose from as you plan your Web site.

Using Text

Text is not the oldest form of human communication, but it's the most efficient for many types of information. It's also what the Web began with. The inventors of the Web were looking for a way to share text files among scientific researchers around the world. These long, technical documents contained only words and numbers—no pictures, no diagrams, no pretty colors. Because text was designed from the start as a fast and efficient way to share ideas among widely scattered audiences, it travels quickly along the Internet.

The language of most Web pages is Hypertext Markup Language (HTML). This system of coding text files for retrieval and display over the Internet was invented when most of the information that was sent over the Internet was text. Many Web pages are full of graphics, animation, and video and have little text, but text remains the fastest and most compact way to communicate a lot of ideas quickly. It takes advantage of the Internet as it was engineered to be used. Most Web sites use text extensively to get their ideas across. Figure 1.15 shows an example.

This page from the Web site of a college course uses text for two purposes: to communicate the content of the news and to help users navigate and execute commands. The only graphic on this page is the college logotype. Notice that the text is carefully designed and laid out so that it's easy to read. It uses a font that is easy for the eyes to follow. There's plenty of white space at the margins. There are no pictures to interfere with the text, which is black on a plain white background.

Reading from a computer screen is not as comfortable as reading from the pages of a book, so it's important for Web site designers to go out of their way to make the text on their Web sites easy to read. In Chapter Four, you'll learn how to choose text fonts and how to design and write text to help visitors read your site's content.

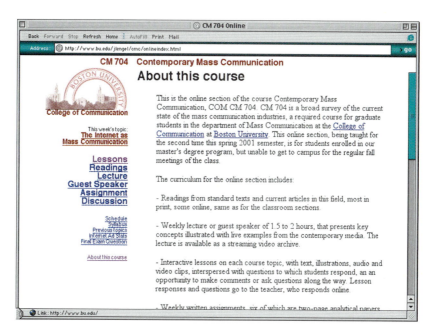

Figure 1.15 Text Page from University Web Site

Hypertext

Notice the words that are displayed in blue type in the article shown in Figure 1.15. When you click this word, you go to another Web page. This feature, called a **hyperlink**, is one of the key aspects of interactivity on the World Wide Web. A number of technologies can be used to implement a hyperlink. Figure 1.5 illustrates one of the most popular: **hypertext**, in which the link is implemented via a word in a text document. As you plan your site, think about how you might use hypertext. You can use it to

⭐ Link to another Web page in your own site

⭐ Link to another Web site

⭐ Link to a spot elsewhere on the same page

⭐ Link to an image on your Web site or elsewhere

⭐ Link to a voice, music, or sound clip

⭐ Link to a video

⭐ Open a new window, perhaps smaller, to display a definition or other information

☆ **DO IT YOURSELF**   **Follow the Links**

To better understand the possibilities of hypertext, it's a good idea to visit some Web sites and follow the hypertext links. Where do they lead? Browse the Web until you find an example of each of the kinds of hypertext hyperlinks described here.

Printing

Some text documents are best read on the computer screen, as regular Web pages, and then printed as necessary. Other documents, especially long, technical documents, are used by most readers in their printed form. If your site presents these kinds of documents, you can display them in Portable Document Format (PDF) format. To read a PDF file, visitors must have the Adobe Acrobat Reader program, which automatically opens and displays PDF files when users click them. The printed quality of PDF files is higher than that of standard Web pages.

Some Web sites include key documents both as standard Web pages and as PDF files, letting the user choose which to view. To see some examples, browse the Web. Download and print a sample PDF file. How does this experience compare with reading a text file on the Web page itself?

Planning for Text

Look at your list of purposes and functions. Which of these can best be implemented through text? For each function, what kind of text will be needed—long, scrolling articles? Short paragraphs that can be read on one screen? Has the text already been written, perhaps for a printed publication of the organization, or will it need to be composed from scratch? These are the questions you need to answer in the planning stage. The answers will help you to lay out the structure of the site and to prepare a list of the items you need to gather.

Images

After text, images are the most frequently used form of information on the World Wide Web. Most Web pages use at least a few images, and some sites are made up almost entirely of pictures and graphics. Figures 1.16 and 1.17 show some examples.

Figure 1.16 shows four images: a company logo and three photographs relating to the products that the site sponsor is selling. Even though the page contains some text, images play the most important role. Figure 1.17 shows a Web page that's composed almost entirely of images, some of them animated, with very little text. Images dominate the title of the page, the navigational devices, the background graphics, and the animated illustration.

In the early days of the Internet, Web designers could use only small images, if they used them at all. Some browsers did not display images well. Most users' connections to the Internet were so slow that downloading a three-inch photograph might take 10 or 15 minutes. As image compression technology has improved, as browsers have matured, and as users' bandwidth has increased, images have become less of a burden to the system and so are used widely.

Figure 1.16 Page from the Dorling-Kindersley Web Site

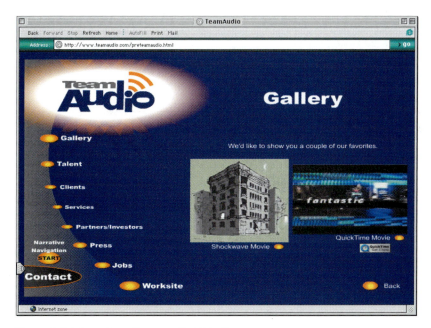

Figure 1.17 Page from Team Audio Web Site

⭐ **TIP**   **Bandwidth and Connection Speed**

Bandwidth is a measure of how much data can flow through the Internet to the user's computer. A low-bandwidth connection is 14 kilobits (14,000 bits of information) per second. A high-bandwidth connection would be 2 megabits (2,000,000 bits) per second. With a low-bandwidth connection, downloading a three-inch photograph might take 20 seconds; with a high-bandwidth connection, about two-tenths of a second. Typical Web users today have bandwidth ranging from 56k (home users) to 512k (office and academic users).

Even with increased bandwidth for many users, you must still consider the cost of using images on a Web page. In the time it takes typical home users to download a small photograph (about four seconds using a typical 56k connection), they could have downloaded four or five pages of single-spaced text. At the bandwidth of a typical modem, a picture is worth about 3000 words.

Images for Navigation

Images can be used to illustrate a story, as in the N.O.A.A. site, or to create a corporate look and feel, as in the Team Audio home page. Images can also be used for navigation, as in the page pictured in Figure 1.18.

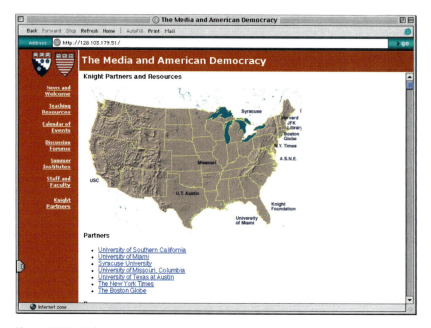

Figure 1.18 Web Page with Image Map

Here, a click on the map takes visitors to the selected site. The image of the map serves as a means of selection and navigation. Images can also take the form of

icons: small images that represent an idea. On the page in Figure 1.18, the two shield-shaped icons represent the two site sponsors.

Most Web sites contain images of various types, each serving its own purpose. Each image is developed separately, usually in a program such as Photoshop. As you specify the functions and purposes of each page in your site, you should include a list of images you'll need.

Most images in a Web site are static, but others can move and change. These images, called animations, are discussed next.

Multimedia

The Web is growing quickly in its ability to support communications using media other than text and static images. **Multimedia** (the term coined to refer to the range of online media available) Web elements are more accessible to more people as their bandwidth increases, and the tools for creating and publishing animation, sound, video, and other forms of interactivity are becoming easier to use. As you consider the possibilities offered by these media, take a look at the purposes and functions you listed earlier for your Web site. Can any of them be accomplished best through the use of multimedia?

To be effective, multimedia elements require considerable bandwidth. Sound and video are especially hungry for kilobits. In addition, music and animations that play themselves unsolicited may annoy users. So before you plan to include multimedia in your site, think about the audience. How many of them enjoy a high-bandwidth connection? How many do you expect will upgrade by next month? By next year? The possibilities for multimedia on the Web are powerful, but only if they fit the situation of your audience and help further the purposes of your site.

Animation

In its simplest form, an **animation** is a series of still images played one after the other to give the impression of motion and change. Animations can be used to capture the eye of a viewer or to illustrate a process. An example of the former is a banner ad on a Web site that flashes "Win $1000!" alternating with "Click here now!" The second type might include a moving diagram that shows the process of photosynthesis in a biology lesson. The first type is easy to create and takes little bandwidth to receive. The second example requires careful development and may take more time to download.

As you think about multimedia for your site, it's a good idea to browse the Web for examples of animation. Almost every site uses some sort of eye-catching animation, but few employ more complex and serious animations. For complex (but not always serious) animations, connect to the Macromedia Flash Web site at http://www.macromedia.com/. Flash is a program used to create complex animations. We can't print animation examples in this book, but you can view several on a short online visit.

Text can be animated, as can shapes, logotypes, drawings, and photographs. Animations can play so quickly that they are hard to see, or slowly to create a somber mood. An animation can stay in one portion of the Web page or move across it. For example, a car dealership site might feature an animation of a car speeding across the screen. An environmental site might show a moving map of the deforestation of the Amazon rain forest. A biography site might show a series of portraits, each dissolving into the next as the subject ages. An educational site might illustrate the process of changing a faucet washer through a multistep animation. How might animation help you accomplish some of the purposes of your site?

In Chapter Five you will learn how to design and create simple animations. At this planning stage, it's sufficient to make a list of the animations that you will need to communicate with your audience.

Sound

Sound is the most primitive of the means of communication. Many animals use sound to communicate what's up. Humans have been speaking to one another from our beginning as humans, probably before we drew pictures and certainly before we wrote books. Music, another ancient invention, communicates feelings and moods in a different way than does spoken language. As Internet bandwidth increases and computers get better at reproducing sound, we will see more voice and music on the Web. In a culture such as that in the United States, where people spend almost half their day listening to television and radio, you cannot ignore the appeal of voice and music to this audience.

Although few sites need to use voice technology to achieve their objectives, you'll find that voice can often supplement text and images to communicate more powerfully with the target audience. For example, voice might be used on a news Web site to broadcast a press conference by a public official. In the earlier example of the animation of the washer replacement, voice might be used to help the home repairer follow the steps one by one. A friendly voice might remind visitors to "Shoot the monkey to win a million dollars!" Clearly pronounced words and phrases can help a student learn a foreign language online.

The use of music on the Web is growing quickly. Some Web sites are all music, such as the radio stations that broadcast live and continuously on the Internet. Others play music on demand, letting you listen to your favorite sonata or popular torch song whenever you wish. To put the viewer into a relaxed mood, a soft Mozart divertimento plays on a Web site for a mountain resort. Hot jazz plays whenever you log on to a New Orleans tourist site. A university's school of music lets you listen to student compositions on its Web page.

To implement sound on the Web you use special software tools. One such tool is Macromedia SoundEdit, which records sound from the original source in a digitized form that can be transmitted over the Internet. Raw sound files are huge, requiring bandwidth of about 100k, so they must be compressed before they are used in a Web site.

☆**DO IT YOURSELF**   **Listen to the Web**

Browse the Web, listening for voice and music. Make a note of how sound is used to communicate the sponsors' purposes. Then go back to your own list of purposes, and note where voice or music might be used to help your audience get the most from your site.

Video

You can think of **video** as a series of still images that are played back rapidly so that they create a feeling of motion, accompanied by a synchronized sound track. That's how video works on television and also on the Web. Video files are even larger than sound files, so to work effectively, video files require significant compression as well as high bandwidth. These technologies are improving swiftly, and Web users increasingly will come to expect to see video as part of the browsing experience. Not all Web sites need video to accomplish their objectives, but the thoughtful Web designer needs to consider the role of this most popular form of multimedia.

It's a good idea to browse the Web looking for video. Organizations such as the British Broadcasting Corporation and ABC News, for example, send a live video stream on their Web sites 24 hours a day. You might also find an online course at a university that includes video archives of guest speakers and lecturers. A manufacturer of kitchen appliances shows key product features using short video clips. You might find a live video Web cam sending video from a water hole on the African savanna to help viewers understand the daily routines of wild animals.

Some people say that the personal computer will replace the television set as the chief means of displaying video in the home. Although this hasn't happened, the technologies are moving quickly in that direction. On the Web, video can be live and continuous, as with television, or users can choose to view video from digital video archives stored on Web servers. In Chapter Five you will learn how video is captured, edited, and compressed for use on the Web. You'll also learn how it is stored on servers, embedded in Web pages, and controlled by users. For now, you should look again at your list of purposes for your Web site with an eye toward determining which ones lend themselves to the use of video.

Virtual Reality

Virtual reality (VR) refers to **panoramas** in which you can enjoy a 360-degree view of a location by moving the mouse as if you were moving your viewpoint. It also includes views of **objects** that you manipulate with the mouse and rotate as if they were in your hand. Producing these forms of virtual reality is fairly easy. They do not take very much bandwidth and can be useful for certain purposes. A real estate site, for example, might allow visitors to step inside the living room of a house for sale and see the view from the picture window. Then users might walk into the kitchen, zoom in on the granite countertops, and spin around to see the lovely cherry cabinets. Many automobile manufacturers give visitors a similar experience from the interior of their latest models.

This technology offers many possibilities. A museum site might provide VR displays of its pre-Columbian artifacts, which Web users can pick up, turn over, and zoom in on to see special carvings. A retailer of high-end sneakers might let potential online purchasers do the same with various models of running shoes. A course on home repair might include an object VR of a faucet valve viewable from all angles.

To find some virtual reality on the Web, a good place to start is by going to `http://www.apple.com/quicktimevr/`. To create these kinds of VR files, you take a long series of still photographs from many different angles and then combine them into a single image file. When this file is viewed with a special software plug-in, the user is presented with an experience that's close to reality. For now, at the planning stage, consider where virtual reality might help your site accomplish some of its purposes.

☆ **TIP**   **Plug-Ins**

For users to see and hear multimedia files, their computers must have **plug-ins**, programs designed for this purpose, installed. For sound and video, the most common plug-ins are RealPlayer and QuickTime. For virtual reality, you need QuickTime or another plug-in. Complex animations may require the Shockwave-Flash plug-in. If you're planning to use multimedia on your site, you must consider whether your target users are likely to have the needed plug-ins.

Interactivity

It's what distinguishes the new media from the old. It's what makes communication responsive and personal. Web designers often speak of the importance of **interactivity**, but they seldom define it.

At its simplest, an interactive Web page involves action on the part of the user, action that in turn prompts a reaction by the computer. Interactivity comes in many forms. At an interactive Web site, a user can do any of the following:

☆ *Choose*: She can select the place she wants to go to or the topic she wants to explore. She can click on a word she wants to know more about or choose the city she wants to fly to. Choosing, the simplest form of interactivity, is inherent in the structure of the World Wide Web. The opening page of the Web site of the *Financial Times*, for instance, lets the reader choose from among a list of sections and stories.

☆ *Animate*: The user can click to see a process in action, learn a concept via a moving diagram, or watch an event occur over time and space. Animations on demand can be used to provide ideas at the time that viewers need them and in the form most appropriate to their understanding. When animation is combined with manipulation (discussed later in this list), the result is enhanced interactivity. On the *Biology Place* Web site, for example, you can learn about the process of cell division by manipulating an animation of typical cells.

☆ *Search and find*: Whenever tools on a site help users to find what they're looking for, the site seems more interactive. A multidimensional menu is a simple form that supports searching and finding. Searching by key word, and then choosing from a list of **hits** (computer jargon for something that matches a search term), is perhaps a bit more interactive. The more open and natural the search method, the more interactive it seems to the user.

☆ *Buy and sell*: Making a commercial transaction—renting a car, buying a book, subscribing to a magazine—is an essential interaction between buyer and seller. As e-commerce grows, this form of interactivity will proliferate. The more direct, quick, and responsive the transaction, the more the user will perceive it as interactive. When buying and selling are combined with searching, finding, and choosing, the result can be highly interactive.

⭐ *Manipulate*: Using the mouse to move things around on the screen is a viscerally interactive process. It allows the user to make complex selections and to see the results immediately. It gives him the feeling that he is controlling the computer and not just reacting to it. To provide a sense of interactivity, this manipulation must be more than the joystick controls found in computer action games.

⭐ *Construct*: In this higher form of manipulation, the user builds something on the screen by making choices, manipulating objects, and selecting alternatives. The result takes shape on the page as she builds it and may even take some action. This most complex form of interactivity puts the user in the role of author, an about-face in communication.

⭐ *Question and answer*: Asking an expert—and getting a response either immediately or later through e-mail—is a satisfying and very human process. Question-and-answer systems extend the function of a Web site to fit the exact needs of an individual user. The answers need not be delivered "live"; rather, the site need only give users the sense that their questions are being answered.

⭐ *Converse:* Talk is a natural form of human interaction. The sense of participating in a conversation is what makes the telephone and e-mail the most popular interactive technologies. Conversation can happen on a Web site synchronously (via chat rooms) or asynchronously (via threaded discussions).

⭐ *Play:* Swiss developmental psychologist Jean Piaget wrote that interactive play is how we build our intellectual capacities. All these forms of interaction can include a component of play. Playing with objects or ideas or people is a good way to get to know them. Play may be the highest form of interactivity, and the wise Web designer will consider this point.

Few Web sites will include all these forms of interactivity, but this list shows the extent of the possibilities inherent in Web technology. The key point is that it's a two-way medium and so offers communication possibilities not offered by television, radio, magazines, and books. As you look for examples of these kinds of two-way interactivity on the Web, think about the list of purposes you generated for your site, and consider where interactivity might help accomplish them.

◎◎ Completing Your Planning Table

You've now completed the planning process for your Web site. You've defined the audience, set forth the purposes of the site, and explored the possibilities for implementing your goals. Now it's a good idea to summarize your plans in an extended table like the one shown earlier. At this point, your planning table might look something like the one shown in Table 1.2.

Table 1.2 Sample Planning Table

Purpose	Structure	Function	Media
To inform its audiences about XYZ happenings	Calendar of Events section: Here viewers will find a listing of various types of events: workshops and institutes; media events; and online discussions and chats offered by the program.	Users can search events by date, topic, and location, or browse a list of all events.	Text, with small icons for each type of event
To educate its audiences about XYZ	Institutes section: This section will display publicity and registration information for summer institutes and other workshops offered by the program and its affiliates.	Users can link to teaching resources and video clips that show the nature of the institutes, and an online application form will facilitate registration.	Text, images of previous institutes, video, online registration form
To promote intelligent conversation about XYZ among all three audiences	Forums section: Viewers will go here to read about new ideas, follow the thread of a topic they are interested in, and compose and post their own two cents' worth.	Users can participate in an asynchronous discussion system as well as synchronous chat discussions.	Text, online conversation

This abbreviated table shows the specifications of only a few of this sample site's purposes and lists only a few sections. No matter which details you include and what form the table takes, it should describe the following elements: the site's purpose, the structural elements, the functions, and the media elements and interactivity.

Now that you know why you are building the site, who will be using it, and which functions it will perform, it's time for the next step, which is to design the site so that it will accomplish its goals. That's the subject of Chapter Two, where you will learn to apply concepts of visual design, navigation, user control, and media display to the creation of your site.

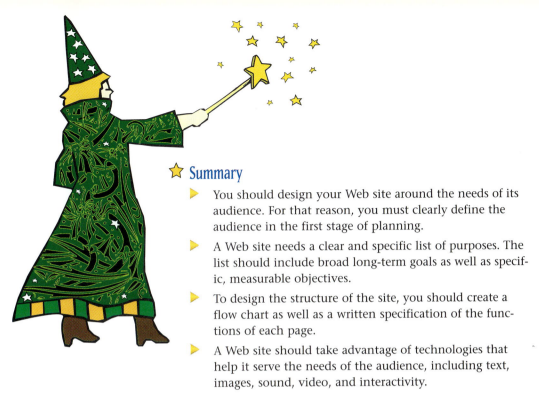

⭐ Summary

▶ You should design your Web site around the needs of its audience. For that reason, you must clearly define the audience in the first stage of planning.

▶ A Web site needs a clear and specific list of purposes. The list should include broad long-term goals as well as specific, measurable objectives.

▶ To design the structure of the site, you should create a flow chart as well as a written specification of the functions of each page.

▶ A Web site should take advantage of technologies that help it serve the needs of the audience, including text, images, sound, video, and interactivity.

▶ When your planning is complete, you should document your design decisions using a table that lists each of the site's purposes and its corresponding structure, functions, and media.

⭐ Online References

WebResults Guide to Web Design. Some principles and suggestions for planning a Web site, from a company that does this for a living.
http://www.webresult.com/webr/des/des.html

Plan Your Site at CNET Builder.com. Straightforward suggestions for defining your audience and stating your mission.
http://builder.cnet.com/webbuilding/07307.html?tag=st.bl.3881.dir2.7307

⭐ Review Questions

1. Name the basic steps in planning a Web site.

2. List at least three ways to define the audience for a Web site.

3. Explain the differences between organization-centered, technology-centered, and user-centered design.

4. Explain the difference between a site's goals and its objectives.

5. Name at least four forms of interactivity that can be used on a Web site.

6. Explain the purpose of a flow chart in planning a Web site.

7. Which Web technologies might best be employed by a site designed to sell compact discs to country music fans? Why?

8. List the different types of media that can be employed in a Web site.

☆ Hands-On Exercises

Create a plan for a sample Web site—an actual site or a hypothetical one. Include the following:

- A definition of the audience: demographics, interests, technical abilities, and computer situation.

- A statement of purpose, including at least three long-term goals and, for each goal, at least two specific objectives.

- A flow chart showing the structure of the site.

- A written specification of the functions of each section of the flow chart.

- A description of each Web technology employed in the site and an explanation of why each should be used.

CHAPTER TWO

DESIGNING DISPLAY AND NAVIGATION

To design a Web site is to find a way to serve the user's needs in the most direct way possible while working within the confines of available Internet technologies. As you work, you take into consideration information theory, principles of learning, the visual arts, computer display technology, and knowledge of human behavior. A well-designed Web site doesn't just look good; it also works well.

Chapter Objectives

- To consider the various ways that text, images, and multimedia can be displayed on a Web page
- To develop systems that allow users to find their way through the site
- To describe methods for collecting user feedback and supporting interactivity
- To understand the role of corporate identity in the design of a Web site

As you learned in Chapter One, the form of a Web site should follow its function. Your design should be based on what the user needs to do at the site. Any other considerations should take second place to this basic principle. So to begin designing your site, you must look first to the functions that you've listed. Most Web site functions fall into one of these categories:

☆ The display of information

☆ Navigation through the site

☆ Choosing, searching, and finding

☆ Feedback and interaction

☆ Communicating the organization's identity

◉ The Display of Information

The information on a Web site can be embodied in any of the forms you learned about in Chapter One: text, images, animation, sound, video, or virtual reality. For example, one function of the XYZ program is to display information for site visitors day by day and week by week. To implement this function, the site displays these happenings in a calendar of events. In the planning stage, the site designer specified that most of this information would appear as text, with a few accompanying icons. So the designer might simply set up a page that lists the items in tabular format with dates on the left and entries on the right, as shown in Figure 2.1.

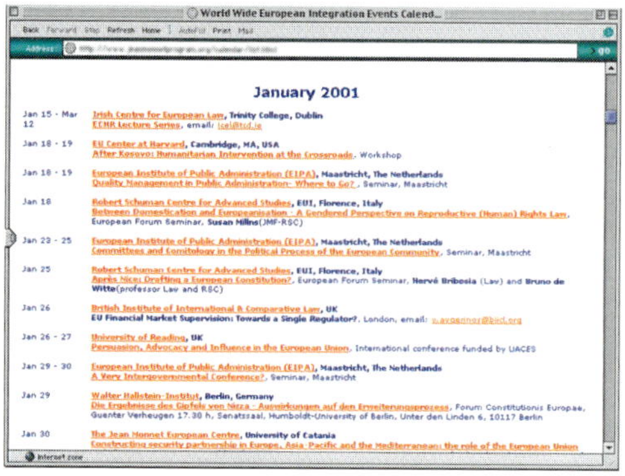

Figure 2.1 Screen Shot of Calendar List Web Page

Figure 2.2 Screen Shot of Calendar Format Web Page

But is a list the best way to display this information? Another alternative is to borrow the format of a paper calendar, with one row for each week and a column for each day, as shown in Figure 2.2.

To decide which display would work best, the designer must walk in the shoes of the user. Does a typical target user think of the XYZ program in terms of a day-by-day calendar that is consulted regularly to see what events are upcoming? Or will most users consult this page infrequently, only when they are looking for a specific event? In every case, the users' needs should determine the nature of the display.

Whichever format is chosen for the calendar, the designer must also consider the site's other functions, such as navigation and communication of the organization's identity. The designer must consider all these functions together in the design of the site. A full consideration of the additional functions might produce a page that looks like the one in Figure 2.3.

Figure 2.3 Calendar List Web Page with Identity and Navigation

The title across the top presents the corporate identity, and the red area on the left side provides navigation to the other parts of the calendar. You'll learn about navigation design later in this chapter. For now, remember that the display of information, like other aspects of site design, takes place within the confines of the site's other purposes.

Reading and Viewing: Text and Images

Most Web sites include quite a bit of text and image information. How should you display them? Should you follow typical magazine design and present the text in two or three columns across the page, with images interspersed? Or should your site look more like a newspaper, with six or seven columns? Or like a book, with one column of text and images placed at the top or bottom of the page? The answers to these questions depend on the purpose of the site, and they are dictated largely by the limitations of the computer display screen.

Early Web designers tried to make Web sites look just like their printed counterparts. A magazine designer might build the display around the format that the printed periodical had developed over the years. The designer for a newspaper's Web site might start with the classic newspaper page. These designs, however, would not work well for the display of information on a Web site. Here's why.

⭐ Typical printed pages are the wrong shape. Magazine pages are taller than they are wide, whereas computer screens are wider than they are tall. A typical newspaper page is 16 inches wide, whereas a typical computer display is about 10 inches wide.

⭐ Typical printed pages use high-resolution print technology. A magazine is printed at a resolution of about 2000 dots per inch, and a newspaper at about 300 dots per inch. This resolution allows the printing of very fine detail in both text and pictures. A magazine set in nine-point type is comfortably readable, so the publisher can fit quite a few words into each square inch of space. A computer monitor, on the other hand, can display only about 75 dots per inch, and in most situations any text set in less than 12-point type is difficult to read.

⭐ Printed documents need not support navigation. Readers of magazines and newspapers do not have to be shown how to go to the next page or how to know when the end of a story is near. And the masthead is always available on the cover or front page to communicate the corporate identity and identify the publication. Web sites, on the other hand, have no built-in navigation or identification and so must provide this kind of information on every page.

> ⭐**TIP**   **Screen Resolution**
>
> *Dots per inch*, *pixels*, and *resolution* all refer to the density of a display medium. A high-resolution medium, such as a book or magazine page, displays about 2000 tiny discrete dots per inch. They're invisible to the unaided eye. A low-resolution medium such as a computer screen can display fewer than 100, and if you look closely you can see them. The higher the number of dots per inch, the higher the quality of the text or image. In Web design, resolution and screen space are measured in **pixels**, which is short for "picture elements." Each dot on the computer screen is one pixel.

Early Web sites sponsored by newspapers and magazines tended to mimic the printed versions. But as Figure 2.4 illustrates, more recent versions reflect the needs of users and the nature of Web technologies.

It would be impossible to display six columns of text on a Web page, so online newspapers use a different form of information design and display. Most of them display a front page that lists only the headlines of each of the major stories. To read the text of the story, viewers click on the headline and navigate to a new page,

Figure 2.4 Financial Times Home Page

where text is displayed in a single column. Site designers have discovered by trial and error that text on a computer screen is easier to read if it's displayed in relatively large type, in a single column about five inches wide, with plenty of white space around the edges.

For online magazine publishers, high-quality images are key. That's why many of them have adopted the **thumbnail** system for displaying pictures. Embedded in the text of a story is a small photo that downloads quickly and does not disrupt the visual flow of the text. It does not show much detail at this size and resolution, but when readers click it, a larger window opens to reveal a higher-resolution, five- or six-inch wide version of the photo, providing much more detail.

Both techniques are examples of **two-stage interactive displays** of information, which rely on the Web's point-and-click interactivity to make them work. Instead of trying to provide all the information on a single page, the Web designer displays a set of headlines or thumbnails on one page. Each of them opens on demand to display the full-resolution text or images that the user is interested in.

> ☆**WARNING** Designing the best way to display text and images is not a simple task, nor can it be modeled on the styles of the traditional media. You must provide for the many functions that a Web page serves, and you must consider limitations of screen resolution as well as the possibilities, such as interactivity, afforded by Web technology.

The Display of Information

☆**DO IT YOURSELF**   **Display Text and Images**

A good way to think about and understand the display of text and images is to review the purpose of one of your site's pages and then sketch out how the text and images might be displayed. Develop at least two contrasting ways to present the information.

Watching and Listening: Sound and Video

Using sound and video on your site presents a new set of display issues. A computer screen does not resemble a radio, and even though it looks like a television set, it cannot display video in the same way. Most computers are used in offices, schoolrooms, classrooms, and libraries, where music and voice emanating from a Web site might not be welcome. Most users want to control the display of sound and video, turning it up or down, skipping forward, stopping the action, or going back to review what they missed. On the Web, they are looking for an interactive experience with these media, which traditionally have been passive pastimes.

On some Web sites, soothing music begins to play in the background as soon as visitors open the page. They have no control over what it plays, or how loudly, or for how long. The music is invisible, with nothing on the page to represent it. Other pages let viewers select a song from a list; the site displays a controller that lets viewers adjust the volume and slide back to the beginning or forward to the end. These two examples illustrate the concept of **user control**, which is key to the display of sound and video on the Web.

Another issue facing the Web designer of sound and video is **embeddedness**. Some sites display video in a separate window, outside the Web page, that contains the controller and other information. This window opens when the user clicks on the video icon on the Web page. When the user is finished watching, he closes the window and resumes browsing the page. Other sites embed video in the page. To view the video, the user clicks the controller. Whether or not to embed is both a design question and a technical issue. Some plug-ins, such as RealPlayer, make it difficult to display video embedded in the page, whereas others, such as QuickTime, make it easy.

Embedded or not, video on the Web is limited in size and quality. To see the current state of the art, visit the Web sites of RealNetworks and QuickTime (see "Online References") and browse through their examples. Video compression and display technology improves daily, and the latest possibilities are always available on these sites. Notice the size, sharpness, and smoothness of the video. This represents the quality that you can expect to use on your own site. As this book is being written, the largest live Web video that can be delivered to high-bandwidth users is 480 pixels wide, quite sharp, and playing at 15 frames per second. Such a video would not quite fill a typical Web page.

For certain purposes, a smaller video may serve your purposes better than a larger, screen-filling video. In the page shown in Figure 2.5, a college offering an online course presents a professor's lecture on a page that contains the text of the lecture on the left, a slide or illustration on the right, and a small head-and-shoulders video of the lecturer in the lower right.

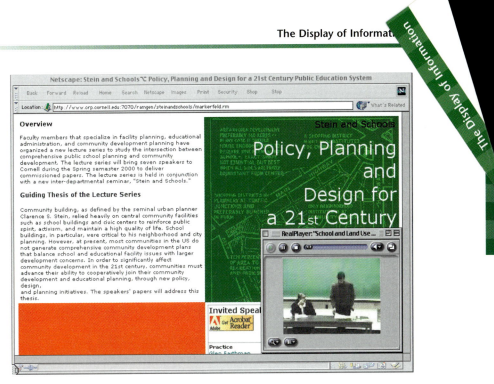

Figure 2.5 An Online Lecture

Making the video, which provides very little visual information, any larger would make the text too small to be useful and would reduce the size of the illustration. If you're trying to decide how big to make a video and whether to embed it, you must consider the nature of the video that's available, how it fits into the site's purposes, and the limitations of current technologies.

As with video, you can embed sound in different degrees.

⭐ You can hide control of the sound from the user. The sound is fully embedded in the page, with no separate window and no controller.

⭐ You can display a mechanism for controlling sound in its own separate window.

⭐ You can embed the sound and its controller into the page, without a separate window.

How you choose to display sound or video should be based on the purpose of the page, the nature of the audience, and the way they will want to use the sound and video information. The size and quality of the sound and video will also be limited by the available server and plug-in technologies, and by the user's bandwidth. Here are some examples of how these considerations might be taken into account.

⭐ A site providing health information to retired senior citizens at home should be restricted to small, short video clips of low quality because of the low bandwidth typical of this kind of home user. To avoid the possible confusion of opening a second window and to better position the video next to the text and images to which it refers, the video should be embedded on the page.

☆ A site providing three-dimensional animations of aircraft engine parts to engineers should display the animation in a separate window, thereby enabling users to reposition and resize it as necessary and making it easier to save. Because this audience is likely to enjoy a high-bandwidth connection and to have installed the latest multimedia plug-ins, this site could take advantage of high-resolution video at a high frame rate and could include the latest 3-D technology.

☆ A site for a record company should provide two levels of sound: short, low-quality clips for home users with low bandwidth and short attention spans, and full-length, high-quality clips for users with faster connections or a willingness to wait for a long download. Both options should be embedded in the page to better preserve the corporate identity and visual style.

☆ **WARNING** For some Web sites, multimedia is inappropriate. Neither sound nor video may help to achieve the site's goals. If you try to include multimedia where it is not called for, you'll only increase download time, tax the users' technology, and distract them from their intended purpose. Plan for multimedia only where it belongs.

☆ **DO IT YOURSELF**   **Plan for Multimedia**

Look through the flow chart of your Web site (see Chapter One), and identify those pages on which sound and video will be displayed. Determine the appropriate way to display the multimedia on each page.

Tables and Lists

Some collections of information are best presented in tables, a format that contains rows (items listed horizontally) and columns (items listed vertically). Others work better as a bulleted or numbered list.

Tables are appropriate for information that must be compared in more than one dimension. Examples include the models and features of various products, and times and station stops for various commuter trains. To the commuter browsing the Web to find the next train to Boston, a table of departure and arrival times at the various stations might be the most familiar and easiest-to-use format. To the student looking for the titles of courses available next term, a simple scrolling list might be the easiest way to see the choices.

One example of a table is the calendar shown in Figure 2.3. It has a row for each week and a column for each day of the week. A table need not display horizontal and vertical lines. For example, the rows of photos often seen in clothing catalogs are tables in which the lines are invisible, as shown in Figure 2.6.

☆ **SHORTCUT**   The Web uses built-in systems for handling lists and tables, making it fast and efficient to display information this way.

Figure 2.6 Screen Shot of Web Page with Borderless Table

Tables are also used to format Web pages into rows and columns like a magazine. You can't see the table on such a page, but the pattern of text and images can be created using an underlying (but invisible) table as illustrated earlier in Figure 2.4.

As you decide where and when to use tables to display information in a Web site, consider the restricted width of the screen. A typical computer display is 800 pixels wide. If you subtract from that the borders and scrollbars of the browser window and any space required for site navigation, you end up with perhaps 500 pixels of width to work with. This leaves a display space of only about 100 characters of 12-point text or numbers, an amount far less than readers are used to seeing in printed tables. If you decide to set up your page using tables, you must think through this restriction.

⭐ **DO IT YOURSELF   Plan Tables and Lists**

Which of the pages in your site would best make use of a table or a list? How many columns are necessary for the display of the information at hand? How might you need to modify this number to meet the restrictions of screen size? What kind of table or list will make the information easiest for the user to understand and compare? The answers to these questions will inform your design for these pages.

In Chapter Five you will learn how to format your data as lists and tables for the most efficient display. At this point, the key is to design the display of the information around the needs of your users and the capabilities of their technology.

If building a Web site is like preparing a meal, what you're doing now is deciding what the dishes will look like on the plates when they're presented to the diner. You're considering the food you have in the larder, the nature of your customers, and the china you have available. You must do this before you start cooking, or you could end up with a filet mignon served in a coffee cup, or a nice Bordeaux sloshing in a saucer. You must think through the design of your table setting at the outset.

Navigation through the Site

A beautiful and efficient display of information is wasted unless the user can find it on the site. In a book or a newspaper, it's easy to find things. Readers use the book's table of contents or index, or they rely on the conventional format of newspaper sections. On a Web site, however, visitors have yet to develop any such common means of knowing where they are, where to go next, where they've been, or what's left to see. This book uses the word **navigation** to describe the functions that help users chart their course to and through the information they need.

If your Web site has only one screen of information, you don't need to consider navigation. Otherwise, you must build a system of navigation from the start. This system must provide, on every page, the answers to the following questions:

⭐ Whose site am I looking at?

⭐ Where am I in the site?

⭐ What else is available at this site?

⭐ Where should I go next?

⭐ How do I find what I am looking for?

On the Web page illustrated in Figure 2.7, can you find the answers to all these questions?

In the site in Figure 2.8, how many of these questions can you answer?

A good navigation design answers all five questions using as little space as possible, in the simplest manner, and without distracting from the display of the main site content. A good navigation system is also consistent across the length and breadth of the site. And like everything else on the site, it is built around the needs and perceptions of the target audience.

Figure 2.7 Good Navigation

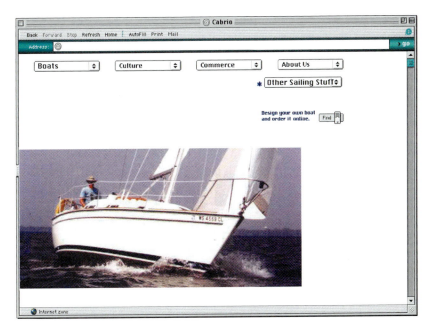

Figure 2.8 Poor Navigation

Identifying the Site

A book has its cover, a newspaper its front page, a television show its station identification. This is how people identify the show or publication. How is this function performed on a Web site? How are users kept informed of whose site they are browsing?

> ★ **WARNING** Remember that users may arrive through a hypertext link from another site and may land on a page deep within your site's structure. How will they know they are on your site unless this information is displayed on every page?

One technique is to display your sponsor's name prominently—for example, in the upper-right corner of each page. If your logo is well known, you can display it by itself.

Most organizations employ a common visual theme in all their publications to identify them to their audiences, and this theme is often incorporated in the Web site. Later in this chapter you'll examine the function of corporate identity in more detail. For now, you should consider how the company colors, font, or logo might be worked into the navigation design.

There are no rules of thumb about where site identification should appear or what it should look like. It can be placed at the top, at the bottom, or in one corner of every page; in large bold type or small letters; as plain text or accompanied by images and logos and colors; as part of a menu bar down the left side of the page, or in a tab system across the top. Your goal should be to provide the necessary function of identification in a way that best meets the needs of the audience. Often, the site identification serves a dual navigational purpose: A click on the identifying logo links the user to the home page.

A site whose purpose is to build brand awareness and corporate identity might display a large, colorful identity item prominently on every page, whereas a site devoted to disseminating arcane research results to a narrowly focused audience of scientists might display the organization's name in small type at the bottom. The first page might devote considerable space to the identity function, leaving less space for the content of the page, whereas the second page might minimize this function to allow more room for content.

★ **DO IT YOURSELF**   **Identify Your Site**

How important is the identity function to your site? How will you show users whose site this is? Sketch some sample pages, trying various approaches to this function.

★ **TIP**   **Print Sideways!**

Web designers who move to the computer from the print world often make the mistake of sketching their Web pages on standard 8.5 by 11-inch paper positioned in the traditional way (taller than it is wide, also known as **portrait mode**). A quick look at your computer screen will reveal that its display is wider than it is tall. If you sketch on paper, place it sideways on the table so that it resembles the form of a computer screen. If you sketch your pages in a word processor, click **Page Setup** under the File menu to orient the page in the **landscape** mode. For details, see Chapter Three.

The site identification information on each page need not provide everything there is to know about the organization, only enough to identify it. Remember that every pixel of space devoted to navigation information is one less pixel available for content. You must balance the need to provide navigation information with the desire to get as much content as possible on the page.

Knowing Where You Are

As you read a book, it's easy to tell where you are, how many pages are left, and which page Chapter Two begins on. When you watch a TV show or see a movie, you know about how long it should last. This navigational information is important to readers and viewers. But Web sites do not have page numbers; nor do they fit within a predictable time duration. Lacking these cues, how do Web site visitors orient themselves within the site? No matter how your site is organized or how many pages it has, you must inform users where they are currently located in the site. Let's look at several techniques.

Menus

In 1984, the Macintosh computer operating system introduced menus, now the most common way of navigating through computer windows. Most Web sites use menus to let users choose where to go and to show them where they are. Menus can stretch across the top of the page, or they can range down the side of the page in a list. Figures 2.9 and 2.10 show examples of these two kinds of menus.

Figure 2.9 Web Page with Horizontal Menu

Figure 2.10 Web Page with Vertical Menu

Menus serve several navigational purposes. They show the categories into which the site is organized, they indicate which category the viewer is in right now, and they let users click to move to another category. Menu items should be short—one or two words—and the number of menu items should be limited. Not every page in the site needs its own menu item.

Menu design and word choice are key parts of the designer's job, and they're harder than they look. The organization and labels of the menu items must make sense to the target audience. Often, you can determine them only by testing the site with users, as described in Chapter Eight.

Consistency and ease of navigation demand that a menu system be identical from page to page throughout the site, so it's important not to design a menu that takes up too much space. Otherwise, it will restrict the space available for content.

If you were to set up a menu system for your site, what would it look like? How many items would there be? What word or words would you use to label each item?

Site Map

A Web site user is more comfortable when she knows how the page she is looking at fits into the larger scheme of things. She wants answers to the questions, Am I deep into the site, or just scratching the surface? Am I near the end of this section? How many more categories like this exist on the site? If I am looking at XYZ, how far away is ABC? You can help a user navigate by providing a **site map** that shows the various sections and identifies the current page.

Designing a site map is not easy. Most Web sites consist of many pages, and to display all of them on a map would take too much space. The flow chart you developed for your site in Chapter One is a site map. Is there space to display this image on every page? It's easy to see why most site maps are displayed on a separate page that is linked to every page of the site. Like a flow chart, a site map shows all parts of the site in relation to each other (see Figure 2.11).

★ **SHORTCUT**   Your site map need not include every page, and it can use two-stage interactive display to allow users to click down to more detail.

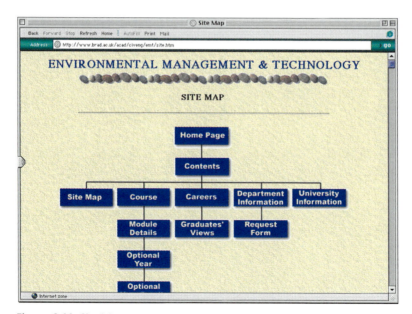

Figure 2.11 Site Map

A site map is not essential to navigation, but it can serve as a useful aid to users.

Cascading Titles

Most Web pages, as well as most sections in the site, contain titles. Starting from the site's home page, users often navigate down through the sections in a search for information. How do users know how far down the hierarchy they've gone?

Many sites use **cascading titles** to show this progression. The progression through an automobile manufacturer's site might look like this:

ABC-Mobile Corp. Home / Products / Sports Cars / ABC SuperCoupe / Specifications

This title, shown at the top of the page, tells users that the current page is Specifications; they're in the section of the site that describes the ABC SuperCoupe, one of the company's many models, which is classified by ABC among its Sports Cars, which are described in the Products section of the site, which is one of the choices on the ABC-Mobile Corp. Home page. Most cascading titles allow users to click on a word in the title to go back up the hierarchy to a previous page.

Look at your site's flow chart. For one of the pages buried deep in the site, write a cascading title in the format just described. Consider how this title would help users navigate. How does it compare with the other forms of navigation you've looked at?

Page Numbering

Not all Web pages fit neatly into a hierarchy. Some, like pages in a book, are designed to be read **serially**, one after the other. In this case, the best navigation aid may be to number the pages and also to display how many pages are left. It must be easy for users to turn to the next page or go back to the page they just read, a function that's usually implemented with Next and Previous buttons. These are the essential navigational functions in a set of serial Web pages (see Figure 2.12).

In your site, will any pages need this treatment? Are there materials that users might want or need to read serially? If so, consider developing a numbering scheme for those pages.

Displaying Choices

On the Web page shown in Figure 2.12, to the right of the page number is a pop-up menu. When it is clicked, it shows the titles of all the pages in the series.

This feature allows users to see what's next, to see which topics have been covered, and to jump back or forward quickly to other subjects in the series. It makes all the choices readily apparent. This helps to answer two of the key navigational questions:

☆ What else is available at this site?

☆ Where should I go next?

No matter which approach you take, you must ensure that all the navigational choices are showing on the page and not buried at the bottom where the user might not see them. It's especially important to keep all navigational information "above the scroll," where it is immediately visible and clickable.

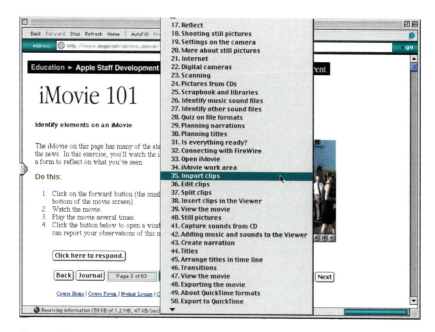

Figure 2.12 Pop-up Page List

Searching and Finding

Sometimes, following a path through cascading hierarchies does not yield the material users are looking for. Perhaps the site map does not indicate the exact location of the desired information, and leafing through a series of pages fails to yield results. Often, such wandering through a site is frustrating to users. You must often provide additional tools to help users answer the question, How do I find what I am looking for?

The most common tool for this purpose is a **key word search**. Suppose a user of the fictional ABC-Mobile site wants to know what size tires are on the SuperCoupe. If the site is equipped with this tool, the user can enter the words *SuperCoupe tires* into a text-entry field, click a Search button, and be taken directly to the specifications page where this information is listed. Many Web sites provide this valuable navigation tool. A similar function can be served with an alphabetical list of topics and subtopics. The user scrolls through the list, clicks on the topic, and is linked directly to the relevant page.

⭐ **DO IT YOURSELF** **Design a Search Function**

Would a search-and-find function improve the navigation of your site? Where should the text-entry field and search button be placed on the page? How much space should they take? Should this feature appear on every page? These are the questions you should consider at this point in the design.

Navigation

Navigation can be a complex task in a Web site. A page that included all the navigational devices described here would have no room left for content. Your task is not to provide every navigational aid to every user on every page. Instead, your goal is to select those functions that will be most useful to the typical members of your target audience. The next step is to arrange them on the page so that they are obvious, consistent, and easy to use while taking as little space as possible. The design decisions here hinge on the nature of the site and user expectations.

When you go to the corner diner for lunch, you read the list of sandwiches from the wall. There is no printed menu because you don't need one. Your choices are clear, and you know what's available. But when you go to a formal banquet, with several courses, assorted vintage wines, and various inspiring speakers, your expectations change. To help you navigate your way through the evening, you expect a multipage, nicely printed menu that details each item in the order it will be served. In both cases, you need a menu, but each has its own form. In the same way, the nature and extent of a site's navigational devices must be designed to match the ways the target audience will use the site.

◎◎ Feedback and Interaction

So far, you've compared your Web site to a book or a magazine—a one-way medium in which the editor displays information to readers to help them find what they're looking for. But the Internet is a two-way medium. It can gather information from users as easily as it provides information to them. The promise of the World Wide Web is to serve as an interactive medium that supports transactions and conversations with and among the users of a site. How does the Web designer support this two-way interaction?

Opportunities for feedback and interaction should be evident in the site's list of purposes. For example, the XYZ site described on page 10 in Chapter One lists as one of its purposes "to promote intelligent conversation about XYZ among all three audiences" and, more specifically, to provide a place where visitors can "read about new ideas, follow the thread of a topic they are interested in, and compose and post their own two cents' worth" on the topics at hand. To accomplish this purpose, the site planner called for "an asynchronous discussion system as well as synchronous chat functions." In the fictional ABC-Mobile site, the designer might call for the user to be able to purchase a new set of tires for an ABC SuperCoupe. The Web site of a record company might provide a way for users to vote on their favorite new artist of the month. All these examples involve collecting information from users, returning it to the sponsoring organization, and then using it to complete some kind of transaction.

Think about the purposes of your site. Do you need to collect information from users? How will you implement this feature?

Web sites commonly collect information from users in two ways: **explicit** collection, which the user is aware of; and **implicit** collection, which the user does not know is happening. An explicit collection, for example, is made when users enter their name and e-mail address to enter a contest. Users type the information and click the Submit button, and the information goes into the Web site's database, where it will be among those drawn from to award the prize. If that same site keeps track of which pages a user looked at, stores that information under the user's name in the same database, and uses this information to market goods and services targeted to the user's interests, that is implicit collection.

At this point, you're more concerned with the explicit collection of information because it requires that you allocate space and program functionality. But you should be aware of the nature of the implicit data that can be collected as users browse the site.

Users "talk back" to a Web site through **forms**, **discussion boards** (also called **forums**), and **chats**. Each of these works in a different way and returns different kinds of data. For instance, to collect the names and addresses of people interested in a certain product, you would use a form. If you wanted to allow users to "follow the thread of a topic they are interested in and compose and post their own two cents' worth" you would employ a discussion board. To conduct live online debates on public issues, you would use a chat.

Forms

The simplest form of explicit feedback is the information collected through a form on the Web page. The user types information into or makes selections on the form, and it is sent to the Web server when the user clicks the Submit button.

Forms can display a number of mechanisms, including text fields, radio buttons, text areas, and check boxes. You will learn how to design and program these kinds of forms in Chapter Five. At this stage, your task is to consider the kinds of information to be collected. Examples include the user's name, e-mail address, and choices of color and style. When the user clicks the Submit button, the information is sent over the Web to a **database server**, which records the data as a new record in a database. Later, the sponsoring organization uses the records in the database.

Discussion Boards

A discussion board lets members of the target audience share ideas and information directly without mediation by the site sponsor. In a discussion board, the user types a comment or a question into a form, clicks the Submit button, and immediately sees the comment displayed on the page. It's like posting a notice on a bulletin board. Anyone else who visits this Web page, now or later, will see what the first user posted.

Discussion boards are an example of **asynchronous communication**, meaning communication that is not bound by time. You can post a comment today, and someone else can read it tomorrow and comment on it next week. Others can read it a month later. Many organizations use discussion boards to promote interaction among audience members and to gather feedback.

If one of the purposes of your site is to promote this kind of communication by the audience, you should consider setting up such a system. Virtually impossible to implement with traditional media such as brochures, magazines, radio, and television, a discussion board takes advantage of the two-way nature of Internet communication to put the audience into an active, participatory mode.

Chats

An online chat is an example of **synchronous communication**; all the participants are online at the same time, and they immediately see and respond to each other's comments in real time. You type your opinion, click the Send button, and, along with everyone else, you immediately see it posted to the Web page. Chats can bring a measure of interactivity to a Web site, putting the audience into a conversational role. A chat is like a conference call except that it's conducted on a computer rather than a telephone and occurs through reading and writing rather than talking and listening.

The site publisher can schedule chats for a particular time and subject or can leave them open and available for members of the target audience to use as they see fit. For a scheduled chat, a Web site might announce, "Tonight at 8:00 PM, in the XYZ chat room, Vice President Calvin Coolidge will discuss foreign policy issues with interested guests. Log in for an exciting hour of online conversation." I can't wait!

During this design phase, your task is to determine which of the site's purposes might best be served through this kind of system.

⭐ **TIP   Text, Voice, or Video?**

It's easy to set up a discussion or chat in text form, where each participant enters comments from the keyboard, and they are read by the others on-screen. But as computers grow in their capability to handle voice and video, will users be able to conduct an online discussion where they can see and hear each other? If everyone in the discussion owns a computer equipped with a microphone and a video camera, they have the necessary equipment, but few people have the required bandwidth and software. Still, a site designer looking to the future must seriously consider implementing such a feature.

◎◎ The Role of Image, Logos, and Corporate Identity

Not all Web sites look the same. A designer goes out of his way to ensure that the site communicates the identity of the sponsoring organization. Most companies and groups have developed a visual identity that's evident in their publications, products, packaging, and other public communication. They might use a symbol or logo, such as the Nike swoosh. They might use a color, such as IBM's blue, to provide a consistent scheme for their publications. Like Apple Computer, they might choose a unique font style for all the text in their brochures, letters, and television commercials. Their radio spots might feature a jingle or special tune. They might use a distinctive shape, such as Ford's oval, in their outdoor signs and on all their products.

A Web site designer must understand the nature and importance of these elements of the organization's identity. All the essential elements should find their way into the site: color, font, logo, and other distinguishing design features, even music. The purpose of extending these identity features to the Web site is to ensure that the audience maintains a clear identity of the sponsor.

Color

Many organizations, including colleges, clubs, companies, and cooperatives, have an official color scheme. Harvard's is crimson, Yale's is blue, Syracuse's is orange, Apple's is red, and Gatorade's is green. In designing your site, you should research your client's existing materials and query the management concerning the corporate colors. Just as these colors are used in other publications of the organization, you should work them into the design of the Web site.

Color is not as simple as it appears. IBM's blue, for instance, is of a lighter shade than Yale's blue. In Chapter Five, you will learn how to program a Web page so that its reproduction of color is as close as possible to your client's expectations.

Logos

Many organizations use a sign or symbol to represent themselves. In most cases, they want this logo to appear as part of the design of their Web site. General Electric, for instance, places its famous circular logo in the upper-left corner of every Web page on its main site and those of all its subsidiaries (see Figure 2.13).

As you design your site, remember that every pixel that's used for logos and other repeated motifs is a pixel that will not be available for content. So it's usually wise to keep the logo as small as possible if it is to appear on every page.

> ☆ **SHORTCUT**   To resize or otherwise work with your organization's logo, ask for the official logo artwork. Many organizations have the logo in digital form.

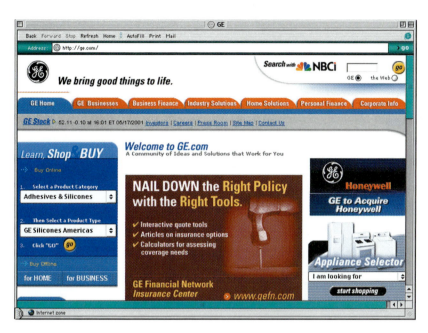

Figure 2.13 The Use of the General Electric Logo

Font

A consistent look and feel is so important to some companies that they specify the exact font to be used in all publications. Usually, this specificity also applies to the Web site. Apple Computer, for instance, has developed its own special font, called Apple Garamond, that is used in all its corporate communications, from magazine advertisements to instruction manuals to Web sites.

You must ascertain the importance of any special font that is used in the Web site. Although it is often impossible to use this font for all the text in the site, the font should appear where the corporate name is included as a page title. For more on choosing fonts, see Chapter Four.

Design Features

Automobiles manufactured by the Ford Motor Company in recent years include many oval-shaped curves in their design. This is one of the ways that Ford distinguishes itself from the competition. This oval design feature is also used in the Ford logo and on the Ford Web site. Notice the use of the oval motif on the Web page shown in Figure 2.14.

You must study your organization's existing publications and products to determine the nature of any design features, like the Ford oval, that should probably find their way into the Web site. These features might include shapes, patterns, an animal mascot, a song, a landscape, or a mountain. In most cases, the client will want this feature worked into the design of the Web site.

Figure 2.14 Ford Web Page with Logo and Oval Motifs

Look and Feel

In the Web site that you're developing, how will you capture the "look and feel" of the sponsoring organization? How will you use color? How will you include the company's logo? Are there any special fonts involved? Are certain design features critical to the organization's identity in the minds of the audience? The answers to these questions will in part determine the design of your site.

Chapter Three delves more deeply into the concepts that will help you develop an even better design, taking into consideration all the factors that lead to an effective Web site.

☆ DO IT YOURSELF   Create an Identity

Go back to the sketch that you prepared earlier in this chapter when you were considering navigational schemes. Now modify this sketch to include elements of corporate identity.

The Role of Image, Logos, and Corporate Identity

⭐ Summary

▶ The display of text, images, video, and sound must be built around the principles of information design and the needs of the target audience.

▶ Navigation information must tell viewers whose site it is, where they are, what else is available, where they can go next, and how to find what they are looking for.

▶ Image, logo, and corporate identity are important aspects of a Web site and must be designed into every page.

⭐ Online References

Web Pages That Suck. Vincent Flanders's opinionated and irreverent site may help you practice good design by avoiding the worst mistakes.
http://www.webpagesthatsuck.com/

Site Navigation from Dmitri's Design Lab. A short article on the basics of navigation. The site also contains other, similar references.
http://www.webreference.com/dlab/9705/index.html

Robin Williams's column in *Eye Wire* magazine. An ongoing discussion of trends in typography.
http://www.eyewire.com/magazine/columns/robin/

⭐ Review Questions

1. List at least three differences between magazines and Web pages in terms of design possibilities and limitations.

2. Sound and video can be embedded into a Web page or viewed externally. Explain the difference between these two approaches.

3. List three situations in which you would use a table in a Web site.

4. What are the five navigation questions that each page must answer for users?

5. List at least three types of menus that can be employed on a Web page.

6. Name three ways to get information from users of a Web site.

7. How can an organization communicate its identity through a Web site?

☆ Hands-On Exercises

1. Draw a site map for a hypothetical Web site. Then draw a sample page, showing menus and other navigation tools that fit the map.

2. Find two sites that have clear and simple navigational tools. Find two sites that have complex navigational tools. Explain the effectiveness of each with regard to its target audience.

3. Design a form for a Web site that will sell subscriptions to a "CD-a-month" service. Include all the items necessary to the order, but try to keep it on one page.

4. Explain the difference in purpose and functionality between a discussion forum and a live chat. Design a chat page and a forum page for the CD company mentioned in Exercise 3.

5. Find a corporate site on the Web, and analyze it in terms of color, logo, font style, and other design features.

TOWARD A BETTER DESIGN

This chapter delves more deeply into the discussion (begun in Chapter Two) of designing a Web site. It sends you off to observe and critique existing sites and develops key design concepts and guidelines. It provides important details on designing text so that it is readable on the computer screen, and on sketching and prototyping a site design before beginning production.

Chapter Objectives

⭐ Understand how existing sites incorporate key design concepts

⭐ Learn how to apply guidelines for good site design

⭐ Learn how to use color, balance, alignment, and other tools to give your Web page eye appeal

⭐ Become aware of the process of sketching, prototyping, and testing your design

◎◎ Observing and Critiquing Existing Sites

Before settling on the design of your own site, it's a good idea to survey the waterfront. By looking closely at other sites on the Web, analyzing how they achieve the objectives described in this chapter, and thinking about how they might do it better, you can inform the design of your own site. The more sites you can analyze, the better informed your own design will be.

For the purposes of your work in this book, you should analyze at least three Web sites:

☆ An existing site from your organization: Most organizations have a site of some kind already on the Web.

☆ A site from a competitor: If you were designing a Web site for the Ford Motor Company, you might analyze the sites of Chrysler and General Motors.

☆ A site from a parallel organization: If you were designing a site for a manufacturer of boats, you might analyze the sites of manufacturers of automobiles.

Your analysis of each site should focus on the design themes and concepts discussed in this chapter. As you observe each site, ask yourself the following questions:

☆ The display of information: How does the site display text, images, and video? How does it incorporate sound? How does it display lists and tables?

☆ Navigation through the site: Whose site am I looking at? Where am I in the site? What else is available? Where should I go next? How do I find what I am looking for?

☆ Choosing and finding: How do I select items to view? How do I search the contents of the site? What kind of site map is provided?

☆ Communicating the organization's identity: How does the site use color? What kind of distinguishing font is used? How is the company logo displayed? What design features are included?

☆ Feedback and interaction: How are forms used? Are discussion forums provided? Are chats available? Are there other forms of feedback and interaction?

☆ **DO IT YOURSELF**   **Incorporating Design Features**

After you have visited and examined some sample sites and considered the topics in this chapter, use these same questions to plan how you will handle these issues in your site.

◎◎ Guidelines for Site Design

Now you're ready to look at the details of laying out your site's pages. Even though there are no hard and fast rules of Web page design, there are some principles that you can follow to make your site easier to read and use. Before you sketch out your page design, consider these guidelines, which are based on traditional design principles as well as the realities of publishing for the computer screen.

Aspect Ratio and Display Size

Not all computer screens are created equal, but they all share some common characteristics. The first is **aspect ratio**, the relationship between the height and width of the computer screen. Almost all computer screens have an aspect ratio of 4:3. This means that they are four units wide and three units high. So a screen that is 12 inches wide is 9 inches high; a screen that is 600 pixels high is 800 pixels wide. (For more about pixels, see Chapter Two.) This means that virtually all your visitors will see your Web pages through a rectangular window that is wider than it is tall, so your design must focus on this window shape.

> ☆**WARNING** Even though users can click arrows to scroll down and see the things that don't fit "above the scroll," it's not a good idea to make users do this. If you want them to see something, include it within a screen having a 4:3 aspect ratio.

Most modern monitors have a **display size** of 800 pixels wide and 600 pixels high. A few old-timers are 640 by 480 pixels, and many of the newest and most expensive monitors can show 1024 by 768 pixels. An ultraconservative designer who wanted absolutely everyone to be able to view the page without scrolling would design a page to fit on a 640 by 480 monitor. On the other hand, a Web site designed for wealthy computer aficionados—who presumably own the largest monitors—might safely design for a 1024 by 768 display size. But most designers design for 800 by 600 monitors.

This doesn't mean, however, that the Web page can be 800 by 600 pixels. Rather, the page must fit within the viewer's browser window. The browser's borders and title bars take up space, leaving a smaller rectangle available for your Web page. Figure 3.1 shows the context in which a typical Web viewer sees your Web page.

For most users, the viewable portion of the screen is really 760 pixels wide and 420 pixels high. At 72 pixels per inch—the resolution of a typical monitor—that's 10.1 inches wide and 5.6 inches high, a few inches smaller than a standard piece of paper held sideways. A good designer fits the display of the Web page into this rectangle.

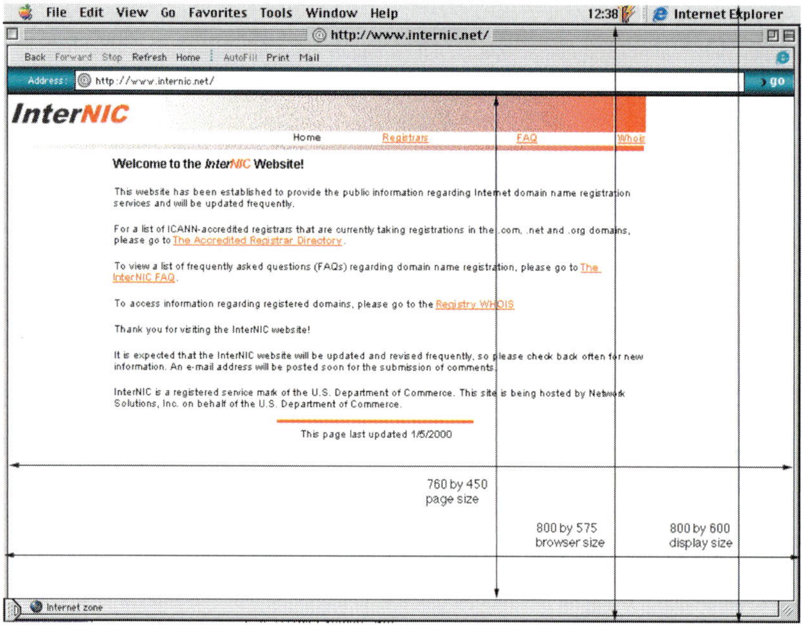

Figure 3.1 A Web Page within a Browser Window

The Roving Eye: Page Layout

When you glance at a Web page (or a book or newspaper page), which part do you see first? Over the years, publishers have learned that the items that appear on the upper-right corner of the right-hand page of a magazine or newspaper are seen first; in other words, the eye of the reader tends to rest there as soon as the page is turned. That's why many advertisers choose to place their messages there. Does this principle apply to Web pages? At this point, all we know is that the top of the page is more likely to be seen than the bottom and that items placed below the scroll are seldom viewed at all. And we know that dynamic items on a page—things that move—seem to capture the eye, at least for a moment.

In addition to location, the number of items on the visible page also influences the reader's attention. Your key message is less likely to be noticed on a Web page that has a dozen visible items than on a page that has only four things to look at. In fact, a cluttered page is disturbing to the eye, often causing users to look away, ignore the page, or go back where they came from.

In short, if you want a certain item or message to be noticed by casual readers, put it near the top of a page that has only a few competing items. It's also a good idea to include a large title or image that makes it clear what the item is about.

Certain items work best in traditional locations. Titles belong at or near the top of the page, mirroring their placement in newspapers, books, and magazines. "Next" buttons work best near the right-hand side because that's where we are used to thumbing to the next page in a book or magazine. Buttons or menu items that take the user up the hierarchy of the site belong at the top because that's the way people think about the organization of a site. "Up" is more general, and "down" is more specific.

Text on a Computer Screen

There is an art to making text on a Web page easy to read. Because of monitors' low resolution, much on-screen text is not nearly as easy to read as printed text. You can't solve the problem of low resolution, but you can go a long way to making the best of what you have to work with. Here are a few guidelines for displaying text:

⭐ Black text on a plain white background is by far the easiest to read. You may be tempted to use the official corporate color as background and to display the text in a contrasting white, but most of your visitors will find the text difficult to read. Our eyes and are minds are used to reading black letters on a white page. This design produces the most contrast and the least eyestrain. It also prints much better on paper. Never display text (that you expect the viewer to read) over a background photograph or drawing. It makes the text almost impossible to read.

⭐ If you look at a well-designed hardcover book, you'll see that the best line length for readability is 10 to 12 words per line. A longer line of text makes it harder for the reader to capture all the words in a single glance and move from one line to the next. Young children and older readers might be more comfortable with an average of 8 to 10 words per line. In Chapter Four you will learn how to program the page to regulate the number of words per line.

⭐ Stick to standard, 12-point system fonts. These fonts are designed to display well on a computer screen and to be easy to read. They have the added advantage of ubiquity—every computer has them, whether Windows or Macintosh, old or new, using Netscape or Explorer. The system fonts include Times, Helvetica, Arial, and Times Roman. Verdana and Georgia are two new font families designed especially for ease of on-screen reading. For the body text of your Web page, it may be better not to specify a particular font, instead letting the user's browser and system configuration choose the most appropriate font for the user's situation.

⭐ Use a serif font for body text, sans serif for titles (see Figure 3.2). The words you are reading right now are set in a serif font. **Serifs** are the little feet and caps on the bottoms and tops and ends of the letters. Times is a serif font. Helvetica and Arial are **sans serif** (without serifs) fonts. Serif fonts are easier to read in standard paragraph text. Sans serif fonts are easier to read in short or single-word titles and signs. In Chapter Four you'll learn how to specify and control font display when you actually program the pages of your site.

In the first forty days

It after forty days with

Figure 3.2 Serif (Top) and Sans Serif Type Styles

☆ To avoid confusing readers, use only two fonts and two sizes on a page. Stick to one font for titles, and another for body text. Make all titles the same size, and make all body text a consistent, smaller size. Twelve-point type displays well on all computers, and for most people is easy to read from the screen. Use this size for body text whenever possible.

☆ Avoid words set in all caps. Use initial uppercase letters to denote the beginning of a sentence, key words in a title, or the name of a person or place. Caps should not be used for anything else on a Web page, except for single-word warnings such as DANGER or STOP. It's easier to read lowercase words because people are used to that convention. Displaying words in all caps makes readers think that YOU ARE YELLING AT THEM.

☆ Make sure that headings contrast with body text. By letting users glance quickly through the material to find the topic they are interested in, headings and subheads make a page of text easier to read. This random-access style of reading is far more prevalent on the Web than in newspapers or books, so you should plan to include more subheads for the screen. To stand out, the headings and subheads should be larger (have a bigger point size) and heavier (be set in boldface) than the body text. Use a contrasting font. If you use Times for the body text, use Helvetica for the headings. Leave extra space around the headings to make them easier to find at a glance.

☆ Separate paragraphs using line space (a blank line) or an indented first line, but not both. Look at a well-designed book and see how the publisher separates the paragraphs. Some use a line space between the paragraphs, whereas others indent the first line. Either method will work on a Web page, but use only one.

☆ Leave plenty of white space around blocks of text. The human eye needs room to roam while it is reading. It likes white space above, below, and especially to the left and right of a column of text. It abhors text that is hemmed in by the edge of the screen, surrounded by boxes, or crowded by graphics. A column 10 words wide with substantial white margins is easiest to read.

⭐ Build your page around a single axis. Our minds seek order and organization. We like things to line up. We read easier if the page is formatted around an **axis**, an invisible line to which the text, images, and graphics align. The axis can be near the left, at the center, or to the right, but the page should have only one.

⭐ Make the page balanced visually from top to bottom and right to left. Don't concentrate the graphics in one corner. Spread things out from top to bottom and side to side in a reasonable way. A balanced display is easier for users to look at and work with.

⭐ Memorize this principle: The simpler, the better. Chaos and clutter are the opposites of order and organization. A simple page with a few visual and text elements is easier to read than a page with a plethora of items competing for attention. Keep the number of items on the page as small as possible. If necessary, divide the contents into two pages. One way to make sure that the user pays attention to your key item is to keep other distracting items away from it, off the page. Figure 3.3 shows a cluttered Web page.

Figure 3.3 Cluttered Web Page

◎◎ Designing for Eye Appeal

As you consider and implement your site design, you should be aware of the impact of color, balance, contrast, alignment, and scrolling. Following a few simple guidelines will make your pages easy to read and pleasing to look at. At the same time, it's essential to keep in mind the importance of user control. Using frames (discussed later in this section) and consistent menus may help your users navigate more easily through the site. And throughout your planning, you should err on the side of simple design and courtesy to your site visitors.

☆ **TIP**   Frames

A Web page built with frames includes two or more separate rectangles, each of which contains its own content, which may or may not change. A common example is a static menu frame on the left-hand side and a frame on the right that displays new content each time a menu item is clicked. At this point, you should consider whether frames will help your users navigate your site and help you display information easily and quickly. Using frames can complicate your programming and confuse navigation for some users. But used carefully, frames can help organize a site.

Color, Contrast, and Balance

In Chapter Two you learned about the importance of color in establishing and maintaining an organization's identity throughout the Web site. Another consideration is how well the color fits with the other elements. Bold, bright colors in menu areas and mastheads distract the eye from other elements, such as text and photographs. Often, it is better to use subtle or pastel colors for these purposes.

☆ **WARNING**   Don't use bold colors or patterns as backgrounds. Text that is displayed over such backgrounds will be very difficult to read. Photographs will compete for attention with the background and will lose their visual appeal.

No matter how you use color, the colors you choose should fit the purpose of your site, and colors used in combination should complement each other. Some colors lend a cool feeling to the page, whereas others warm it up. Some colors just don't go together. A bright blue logo on a dark orange background, for instance, will cause most viewers to cringe. Although it's beyond the scope of this book to develop the entire theory of color, the color wheel will help you avoid the most glaring combinations (see Figure 3.4).

The wheel is built around the **primary colors**: red, yellow, and blue. They're called "primary" because you can build all the other colors by combining them. The secondary colors are the combinations of two of the primaries: orange, green, and violet. You can use the color wheel to help you select colors that fit your purpose and combine well with each other.

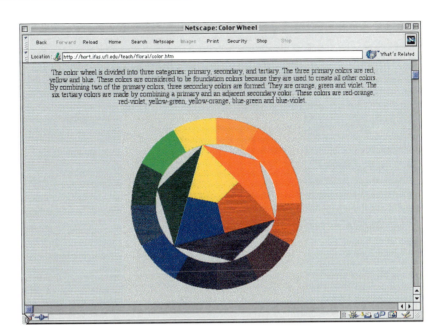

The color wheel is divided into three categories: primary, secondary, and tertiary. The three primary colors are red, yellow and blue. These colors are considered to be foundation colors because they are used to create all other colors. By combining two of the primary colors, three secondary colors are formed. They are orange, green and violet. The six tertiary colors are made by combining a primary and an adjacent secondary color. These colors are red-orange, red-violet, yellow-green, yellow-orange, blue-green and blue-violet.

Figure 3.4 The Color Wheel

For instance, the colors on the left in Figure 3.4—blues, greens, and violets—are *cooler* in tone than reds, yellows, and oranges. The warm colors get their influence from their connection with fire, whereas the cooler colors remind us of the sea and the sky. To some people, cool colors seem more businesslike and detached, whereas the warmer colors seem more fiery and provocative.

Colors that sit directly across the color wheel from each other are called **complementary** colors. Combining two complementary colors makes each seem more intense and brighter, creating a great deal of contrast. That's why a blue-on-orange Web page seems jarring. Colors next to each other on the wheel create less contrast. To create contrast, you can use shades and tints of a single color. Adding black to the color is called a **shade**; adding white is called a **tint**.

There is no "right" or "wrong" color scheme. The point here is simply that some combinations create visual contrast and discord, whereas others induce a sense of comfort and harmony. What kinds of colors will you use in your site? How does your selection of colors fit with the purposes of your site, and with the experience of the intended audience? How would you explain your choices based on the color wheel? These are the key questions at this stage in your design considerations.

☆ **TIP**   **Colors on the Screen**

On the display and in computer memory, each pixel is represented by a number that signifies color and the brightness. For example, a dark red pixel is CC0000 (that's a hexadecimal, or base 16, number), and light blue is 6699FF. All computers and browsers use this system, which allows thousands of different colors. You can play with the colors and numbers at `http://www.visibone.com/colorlab/`.

☆ **DO IT YOURSELF**   **Develop a Color Scheme**

Visit some of your favorite Web sites, and study how they use color. Look for corporate colors, shades and tints, primary and secondary colors, and complementary colors. You may be surprised at the variety of approaches. Next, determine the color scheme for your own site. Later in this chapter, you'll prototype your colors.

Alignment

The human eye likes it when things line up. For example, it wants to see the left edge of a picture line up exactly with the left edge of the text column in which it is embedded. The eye wants the elements of a Web page to be positioned so that they follow a single axis.

For ease of use and consistency, the scheme of alignment for your site should be the same from page to page. A simple page—perhaps consisting of a single column of text and a few images—will form a natural axis along the left margin, where each line of text begins. Because we read English text from left to right and because Web browsers cannot justify text against both left and right margins (that is, space out the text out so that it lines up straight on the right), you'll end up with "flush left, ragged right" columns of text on your Web page. Usually, you must use this left column edge as the core of your alignment scheme. In a book, newspaper, or magazine, where typesetters can align text along both sides of a column, the designer has more freedom in laying out the page.

The sketch of your Web page design, which you will develop in the next section, begins with your choice of alignment schemes. At this point, a visit to your favorite Web sites, with an eye to how the elements are aligned, will help you to think about your own design.

Frames, Menus, and Scrolling

Most Web pages consist of a single frame, but others divide the browser window into two or three areas that can change independently. The page in Figure 3.5 uses three frames: one for the title along the top, another for the list of menu items down the left side, and a third for the content of the page. The top and left frames seldom change as the user navigates the site, but the content frame changes at every click. When the user scrolls through a long document in the content frame, the title and the menus do not scroll up and out of the way, but remain where they were, always available.

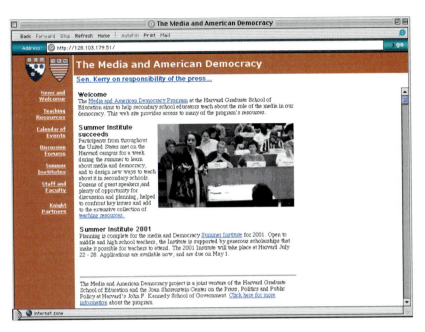

Figure 3.5 Web Page with Three Frames

By using frames, you ensure that

 The main menu items are always available to users

 The menu items always appear in exactly the same place in the browser window

 The title is always present to answer the navigational question, "What site is this?"

 The graphics (in this case, displayed in red) do not reload and flash onto the screen every time a new content page is called up.

Menus

In Chapter Two you learned the importance of providing users with information to answer these questions:

 Where am I in the site?

 What else is available at this site?

 Where should I go next?

In most Web sites, these questions are answered through a **menu** that lists navigational choices. As in a restaurant, the menu lists the items that are available and lets the customer choose which to enjoy next. Not all menu items will be clicked, and not all users will visit the various sections in the same order. A good Web designer makes it easy for users to view the menu, perhaps by keeping it always visible, as in Figure 3.4, or by making it only one click away. A menu can be displayed across the top, at the bottom, or down the sides, but it's best if it shows up in the same place on all pages within a site.

Usually, the menu cannot list every page on the site, so it lists the site's main sections. Then each section displays a submenu of its pages. Your menu scheme depends on the site's size and organizational pattern and on the needs of the typical user. The task now is to place those menu items on the page in a consistent way.

> ☆ **SHORTCUT**   To analyze your site's navigation, use the flow chart you created in Chapter 1.

Principles of Scrolling

As you read this book, you read each page and then turn to the next. This is a familiar and comfortable way to read. The text stays still, and it's easy to keep track of where you are. But on many Web pages, visitors are expected to scroll down through the text to follow the story. To continue reading, they must follow these steps.

1. Grasp the mouse.
2. Take their eyes off the text to find the little scroll arrow.
3. Press the mouse button.
4. Use the mouse to scroll down the screen, trying to follow the text with their eyes as it moves quickly out of view.
5. Release the mouse, hoping they did not go too far.
6. Move their eyes back to the text.
7. Locate the place they stopped reading.
8. Resume reading the story.

This is a most unnatural and inefficient process. You can see why few users ever get to the materials that lie below the scroll.

The computer screen is more like a television than a newspaper. What if the anchor on the evening news, after showing the first story, told the viewers to get up off the couch, walk over to their televisions, and click on the screen to scroll down to the next story? Then repeat the process five minutes later to see the weather report? This would not be considered user-centered design.

> ☆ **DO IT YOURSELF**   **Consider Scrolling**
>
> As you design your Web page, consider how you will handle scrolling. You might build the site like a book, with each screenful of text as a separate Web page that users leaf through as if turning book pages. Or you might require scrolling only for text that only a few dedicated users will need to consult. In no case should essential items of navigation, such as menu items, appear below the scroll.

User Control

Viewers of the nightly news have little control over which story comes first, how long it lasts, or whether the weather comes before or after the sports. All users can do is to click to another station. A novel, on the other hand, provides a modicum of user control within the confines of the serial narrative: The reader can read the last chapter first, but it might ruin the story. A newspaper offers a bit more user control. Readers can scan the headlines, read an entire story, or go right to the travel section and ignore the front page. A Web site should offer as much control as possible, letting visitors choose what to view, in any order, at any level of detail. The Internet is an interactive medium, and user control is a central aspect of this interactivity.

If a Web site were a restaurant, it would be a 24-hour, all-you-can-eat buffet rather than a multicourse *prix fixe* banquet. The sign on the wall would read, "Life is short, start with dessert." The buffet line would remain open, and you would be allowed to return whenever you wished. No one would scold you if you helped yourself to both pasta and risotto. An effective Web site is like that. It lets visitors choose from any of the pages, in any order.

Simplicity and Courtesy

This chapter has presented a myriad of design issues that must be considered all at once, from principles such as color and alignment to options for site navigation. Using all the available options on a single Web page can result in a complex presentation. But most users seek simplicity. When confronted with a page full of diverse colors and choices and frames and menus and text and images and links, they are taken aback and often confused. A complex, cluttered Web page is not courteous to users.

Courtesy can breed satisfaction, and a satisfied user is more likely to harbor positive feelings toward the Web site and the organization that sponsors it. To be courteous, you must distill the complexity of design options into a simple presentation that makes sense to the user at first glance. It's no easy task to design a page that seems simple and straightforward to users and yet takes into consideration the full gamut of design options mentioned in this chapter. Good design is more art than science. In the next section, you will practice this art as you sketch and prototype the design of your site.

Ask a Web Designer

Before we get to the details of your site design, it's helpful to listen to the voice of experience. Following is an interview with Leigh Chodos, President and Web Consultant, Seven Oaks Productions.

Leigh, describe the work you do.

I am a user interface Web designer. I create the beginnings of a site map, then work in a design phase with screen shots and color scheme, then work the design into an HTML template. It's really a rapid prototype of the site. You could say I'm a rapid prototyper.

What are the more challenging aspects of your work?

The clients. Clients need to have a clear idea of what they want. My last client, Morgan Stanley, needed some help to understand who the audience is for the site, what their needs are in regard to the content of the site, and what they are going to be using it for. For instance, the audience for this site was information technology professionals. So we know that they have high-speed Internet connections, big displays, and lots of memory on their computers. So as I designer I can do lots of things. The content was dry, so we used lots of white space to make it easier to read. We avoided clutter with this white space. We made the column of text about four inches wide, which we know is the easiest way to read on the screen.

How do you get started designing a Web site?

We first design a simple site map. It was my job to work with the client to break down his ideas to a manageable site that the users could understand, for smooth and easy navigation. The key word is *simple*. I met with the client for several hours to define what the purpose of each section of the site was, what they wanted to convey to the audience. At first, the client had an idea for a very complicated display of information. They hired us to help them categorize and simplify it. We designed, for instance, a Feature section, put the items into it, presented this to the client, and then they talked about it and agreed. It was like we took their messy apartment, neatened it up, and then said, "Is this what you want?"

How do you try out your ideas?

I use Photoshop as a drawing board and try to work up the "feeling" of their site. This client wanted an open feeling in the site, not "corporate," but jazzy. So I took those ideas and experimented. I built three or four designs or screens, and I tried things out, like angles and colors, that I am not sure they would like. Then I met with the client and sifted through the sketches. The second phase is to take what they like and refine it even more. Once we finalize the design, we agree on a site map, and then I build the first template from the site map and the screen shot.

Now we have a working, one-page plan of the site. Once the client approves that plan, I build the site, which I call the *architecture phase*. I organize the content so that others can understand it. I set it up so that others can put in the content, without me being there.

How would you describe the nature of your work?

Fast paced. It's fun when I have more room to do what I can, and where I can wear lots of hats and work on multiple phases. I get to use my design skills, my business knowledge, my project management skills, and my Web development skills and bring them all into harmony.

◎◎ Sketching, Prototyping, and Testing the Design

To paint the Mona Lisa, Leonardo da Vinci didn't just sit down one day and start painting. Instead, he began by making a lot of sketches. His masterpiece arose not from a single burst of inspiration but from a series of practice drawings, charcoal studies, and sketches. He sketched on the backs of envelopes and scraps of paper. If you want to create a masterpiece, you should follow his lead. Now that you've considered all the concepts described in this chapter, it's time to try out your design, first with some sketches and then with a prototype. Your site visitors will never see your sketches and prototypes. They'll view only the final product. The sketches and prototypes are private, to be seen only by the site designer and close advisers, and are subject to change. In fact, keeping the prototyping process informal, quick, and sketchy may encourage you to make changes and consider a wider range of alternatives.

Creating a Sketch

The first step is to create a sketch. In Chapters One and Two you worked with site identity and image placement and made some preliminary sketches. Take a look at those sketches now, but do not feel bound by them. You have many more concepts to consider now than you did when you made those. The sketch you're making now must take into consideration all the design concepts you've studied:

⭐ The display of information: text, images, sound, video, tables, and lists

⭐ Navigation: menus, identification, and user control

⭐ Feedback and interaction

⭐ Corporate identity

⭐ Location and type of text

⭐ Color, contrast, and balance

⭐ Frames and alignment

⭐ Scrolling

You must also keep in mind the overarching principles of simplicity and courtesy.

Because each page in a Web site has its own purpose, the design of each page may be unique. So you'll be developing several sketches. From your site flow chart (see Chapter One), select certain key pages to sketch, including at least one high-level navigational page and one low-level content page. Then sit down to sketch. Some people find it easiest to sketch with pencil and paper, whereas others use software tools.

Sketching on Paper

This is the easiest and most flexible method, but the results are not easy to duplicate or distribute. Take a plain piece of 8.5-inch by 11-inch paper, orient it sideways, mark off a rectangle 10.1 inches wide and 5.6 inches high, and with a soft pencil sketch out one of the pages from your flow chart (see Figure 3.6). Include all the elements of the page: logos, menus, titles, frames, graphics, columns of text, images, videos, and aids to navigation. Don't be afraid to try things out, change your mind, use the eraser, and redo the sketch. Don't be afraid to crumple the paper, throw it away, and start the sketch over again.

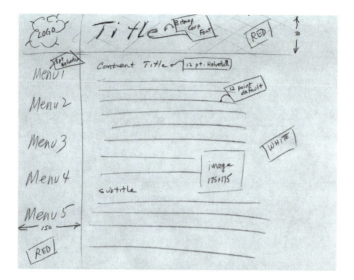

Figure 3.6 Paper Sketch of Web Page

Sketching with Microsoft Word

To create a sketch that might be easier to comprehend and can be distributed electronically, consider using your word processor. The ubiquitous Microsoft Word contains all the tools you need to create a sketch of your Web page, and the results are easy to transmit and share.

Here is how to get started:

1. Open Microsoft Word.

2. Create a blank document.

3. Click Page Setup from the File menu.

4. Set the page orientation to landscape mode (sideways, wider than it is tall).

5. Click OK. Your wide page will appear in the window.

6. Click Page Layout from the View menu. This allows you to see the edges of the page.

7. Click Zoom from the View menu.

8. Click Whole Page from the Zoom to... list.

9. Click OK, and you will see the page on the screen ready for your sketch.

It's tough to sketch freehand with Word, but it's easy to draw simple shapes using the drawing tools. If the palette of drawing tools is not visible, click Toolbars from the View menu, and then click Drawing. The set of drawing tools includes lines, arrows, rectangles, ovals, text boxes, and word art along with tools to modify the thickness and color of each of the objects that you create with these tools.

The purpose of the sketch is simply to show where the basic elements of the Web page will be placed, not to develop a publishable product. Use the tools to lay out the elements on the page, and then modify the sizes and colors of the elements as necessary. A completed sketch might look like Figure 3.7.

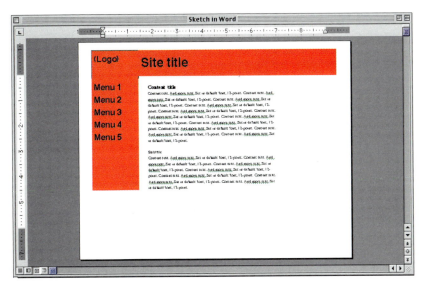

Figure 3.7 Sketch of Web Page Built with Word

To share this sketch, you can print it, attach it to an e-mail, or post it on a file server.

Sketching with Photoshop

If you're sketching a page that contains visual elements such as photographs, backgrounds, and subtle color, the best tool might be Adobe Photoshop or another image-development program such as Quark Xpress or Adobe Illustrator. To begin sketching, you define the size and shape of the page in pixels. In Photoshop, you would follow this process:

1. Click New from the File menu.
2. Set the document size to the dimensions you chose earlier for the Web page (see the section "Aspect Ratio and Display Size"). The most common size is 760 by 420 pixels.
3. Click OK. The window will open.
4. Use the Photoshop drawing tools to sketch the elements on the page.

Photoshop gives you much more control over color, gradients, photos, and text style than does pencil and paper or Word. As with Word, a Photoshop sketch can be e-mailed, posted to a server, or printed.

Adding Callouts

Often, a sketch alone does not fully describe the nature of your design. You may want to develop a second version with callouts that explain certain key features. A **callout** is a text box, linked to the element with an arrow, that gives reviewers extra information about the item. Only the designer and the reviewers see the callout; it is not intended for the audience. You can add callouts to a paper sketch, a Word document, or a Photoshop picture. Figure 3.8 shows the addition of callouts to a picture done in Photoshop.

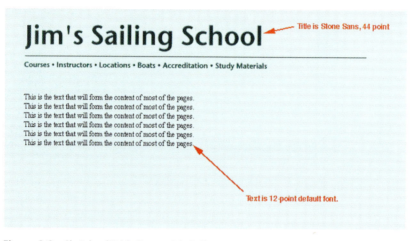

Figure 3.8   Sketch of Web Page with Callouts

It's a good idea to save a copy of the sketch without callouts, along with the annotated version.

Testing the Sketch

A Web designer seldom works alone. Most Web sites are public documents published by an organization for an explicit purpose and viewed by a defined audience. The wise Web designer will run the sketch, at this preliminary stage, past an informal review panel of colleagues, the client, and the audience. This testing of the design concepts can provide valuable feedback at a stage when it is easy to make changes. Here are the steps involved in such a review.

1. Identify the reviewers. Include at least one trusted colleague, one person from the sponsoring organization, and one member of the target audience. All three groups should be represented, but the most important is the user.

2. Explain the purpose of the site. To give a useful response, reviewers should know the purpose and audience of the Web site. A copy or summary of the statement of purpose and the audience definition (see Chapter One) can be helpful. If the site or the page is illustrating a special function or purpose, it's also a good idea to spell that out.

3. Create a package containing the explanation of purpose, the audience definition, and the sketches of the pages, both with and without callouts. In addition, include a list of questions to guide the feedback. The best questions are specific and yet open-ended. "Did you like the sketch?" is not open-ended, and the answer will not be helpful in revising your design. Better questions might be "How does the color scheme fit with the XYZ company's image?" "What might be added to this page to make it easier to navigate?"

4. Make it easy to respond. Your reviewers are doing you a favor, so you should make their task as easy as possible. Send a preprinted review form with the questions, along with a self-addressed stamped envelope if appropriate. Or post an online form where they can write their responses. Be willing to take a phone call and listen to them dictate their feedback.

5. Deliver the package to the reviewers. If you developed your sketches with Word or Photoshop, you can deliver the package by e-mail.

6. Thank the reviewers. Even if they pan your site and tell you to go back to the drawing board, thank the reviewers in writing for their work and their suggestions.

7. Read and consider all suggestions. No matter how outlandish or negative they are, you must consider all of them. You need not follow any of them, but you must think through why the reviewer might have made the suggestion and how the problem that she saw might be solved. One reviewer may say the page is too light, and another, too dark; this may mean that the color is about right. Consider all suggestions, and follow those that help your design better achieve its purposes.

8. Revise the sketch. Make a new sketch incorporating the changes you accepted from the reviewers. Modify the callouts as appropriate. Don't be afraid to make substantial changes, and take the time necessary to revise all the elements that deserve it. At the same time, do not feel bound to respond to every comment and suggestion made by every reviewer.

9. Test again if necessary. A substantial revision calls for a new set of reviews, perhaps by the same people or by others similarly situated. Change the review questions, if necessary, to gather more targeted comments. A minimal revision may not need another test at all, and you can move to the prototyping stage.

10. If you aren't giving the reviewers a second look or if you make changes later, tell the reviewers what you changed. Consider them a part of your Web

development team. Keep them posted on how their comments were considered, and inform them of the revised design. You will need their help later in site development, so it's a good idea to let them know how their suggestions were taken into account.

You've captured your design in your sketches, and it's been tested with the client and the target audience. Now it's time to make the design real by building a prototype of the site.

Prototyping

More than a sketch, a design prototype is a pixel-by-pixel model of the page as users will see it. A prototype is built on the computer and displayed in the same manner as its published form. Like the sketch, the prototype is a test of your design ideas, but in more detailed and realistic form. For small projects, you may want to skip this step, but for anything substantial and professional, a prototype is a necessary—and often time- and money-saving—step in building the site.

The purpose of a design prototype is not to create a working Web site. Instead, your goal is to see whether the design fits the needs of the users and the sponsors.

Prototyping Tools

To develop prototypes, most Web designers use a WYSIWYG ("what you see is what you get") Web page editor or Photoshop. For sites with lots of animation or interactivity, a designer might use Macromedia Flash or Director. The tool you choose depends on the nature of the site and the your familiarity with the tool. This is a rapid prototype, so it may be more efficient to choose a tool you know how to use rather than take the time to learn one that might in theory be more appropriate.

> ☆**TIP**   **WYSIWYG**
>
> With WYSIWYG Web page editing software, you paste the elements of the page into the window of the editor, and it creates the underlying HTML or JavaScript code without your ever seeing it. The editor shows the pages as they will appear to users. Examples of WYSIWYG editors are Macromedia Dreamweaver, Microsoft FrontPage, and Adobe GoLive. In Chapter Six, where you choose the tools for building your site, these programs are covered in greater detail.

Using a Web page editor, you lay out the overall design of the page as a table or grid and then paste into it the graphics and text for the sample prototype page. The file created by the WYSIWYG editor can be read by standard Web browsers, and it appears to viewers in exactly the same form as the fully developed site.

Using Photoshop, you create a new blank document having the exact pixel dimensions of the target window size. Into this document you paste your graphics and text. Most often, the files are saved in JPEG or GIF format so that they can be read by standard Web browsers, thus giving you a look at how the page will appear to the typical user.

⭐ **TIP**   **File Formats**

JPEG and GIF are standard formats for image files. JPEG stands for Joint Photographic Experts Group, and GIF stands for Graphics Interchange Format. These formats describe specific ways to save and compress the data in an image that will be used on a Web page. In Chapter Four you will learn how these formats work and how to choose the appropriate one.

Using Director or Flash, you create a new blank document having the exact pixel dimensions of the target window size. Then you import the text and graphic elements into the program and place them in the proper locations. Then you can use Director's and Flash's tools and scripts to add animation or interactivity. You then save the document in Flash or Shockwave format, which can be read by standard Web browsers.

Creating and Testing a Prototype

To create a prototype, you begin with the revised sketch of one or two sample pages. Then you test the pages with members of the target audience. Here are the steps:

1. Locate the revised sketches of the pages you want to prototype. Use two or three different kinds of pages that incorporate different design features.

2. Using your prototyping tool, replicate the sketch. You may need to build graphics with Photoshop or compose text in a word processor. Include all the elements. Each prototype page should be complete with all the menus, images, titles, footers, graphics, and other elements called for in the design.

3. Test the prototype with members of the target audience. Don't simply show them the prototype and ask them whether they like it. Instead, ask them specific questions, either in an oral interview or in a written questionnaire. Base the questions on the key concepts of Web design that you've learned in Chapters Two and Three. A sample list of questions follows.

4. Revise the prototype as necessary and, if indicated, test it again.

Following is a list of questions to ask your prototype reviewers.

⭐ The display of information: Describe the readability of the text. How clear and useful are the images? How well could you find information in the lists and tables?

⭐ Navigation through the site: Is it clear whose site you are looking at? Can you figure out where you are in the site? Do you know what else is available at this site? Is it clear where you should go next?

⭐ Choosing and finding: Are all your menu choices evident on this page? Where would you click to search and find other items on this site?

★ Communicating the organization's identity: Who do you think sponsors this site? How can you tell? How does this page use color? Is the type readable and pleasing? How is the company logo displayed? What design features did you notice?

★ Design issues: What seems missing from this page? What could be eliminated? On a continuum from simple to cluttered, where would this page fall? What did you notice first on this page?

★ What changes do you recommend? Why?

Next Steps

Armed with a prototype design approved by sponsors and users, you are ready to begin building the site. Chapter Four takes you through the process of gathering the various elements of the site—text, pictures, sounds, and video clips—and then getting them into the proper form for inclusion in the site.

⭐ Summary

▷ To become aware of design issues, it's a good idea to carefully and closely study existing Web sites, applying specific criteria for display, navigation, searching, identity, and interaction.

▷ An effective Web site design incorporates an understanding of aspect ratio and display size as well as page layout and text display.

▷ Simple Web designs that pay attention to color, contrast, balance, alignment, and scrolling are effective and easy to use. You should also pay close attention to the use of frames, menus, and scrolling so that your site presents a courteous face to visitors.

▷ When you've completed the site design, it's important to sketch and prototype your design concepts and then test them with the target audience.

⭐ Online References

Web Content Accessibility Guidelines. This working paper from the World Wide Web Consortium helps you design a site that's accessible to people with disabilities.
http://www.w3.org/TR/WAI-WEBCONTENT/

What Makes a Great Web Site? From webreference.com, this short article is full of ideas and guidelines for good design.
http://webreference.com/greatsite.html

Art and the Zen of Web Sites. A provocative set of guidelines and observations that will make you think twice about your design.
http://www.tlc-systems.com/webtips.shtml

⭐ Review Questions

1. Explain how aspect ratio and display size affect the design of a Web page.

2. List four guidelines for displaying text on a Web page so that it is easy to read.

3. List three issues that the Web designer must consider when choosing colors.

4. Explain why scrolling is an important consideration in page design.

5. List three reasons to sketch the Web page design before implementing it.

6. List at least four steps in testing your design.

7. What are some page sketching and prototyping tools commonly used by Web designers?

8. Explain where frames might be used in Web site design.

☆ Hands-On Exercises

1. Using the list of questions in this chapter, analyze at least two Web sites in different fields.

2. Connect to a sample corporate Web site and view it at three different display resolutions. Explain how variations in resolution affect the functionality of the site.

3. Find some Web sites that (a) display paragraphs of text on a background that makes the text difficult to read, (b) use a font size or style that is difficult for you to read, (c) run the text right up to the edges of the window, leaving little white space in the margin, and (d) clutter the page so much that it is uncomfortable to read.

4. Find sites that do the opposite of each item in Exercise 3.

5. Prototype a "hot" color scheme with lots of contrast. Then prototype a "cool" scheme using calming colors.

6. Sketch a sample page for a Web site, adding callouts to explain your navigation, color, text style, and overall page balance decisions.

CHAPTER FOUR

Gathering and Preparing Text, Numbers, and Images

This chapter explains how to locate, gather, and prepare the basic elements of your Web site: text, numerical information, and images. It covers the available software tools and the file formats that work best for each one. Along the way, it deals with copyright issues, editing tools, and color depth. Your Web site is only as good as the individual items that form its content. This chapter shows how to shape each element so that it contributes optimally to the site's purposes.

Chapter Objectives

- To analyze your Web page to determine its component elements
- To learn the techniques for preparing text to be used on your Web site
- To learn the techniques for preparing numeric data for display on your Web site

⭐ To understand the tools and techniques for editing and preparing images

⭐ To become aware of copyright issues in the preparation of materials for Web pages

◉◉ Listing the Elements

When you've completed the design of your site, it's time to prepare the content. Your site may contain dozens, or even hundreds, of pictures, sounds, videos, logos, and paragraphs of text. Each of them must be gathered and prepared separately. This process takes more of a Web developer's time than any of the other tasks.

The first step is to make a list. Using the site's flow chart (see Chapter One), you develop a list of the elements for each page. The list describes each image, video, graphic, sound, or column of text that will appear on the page. To get an idea of how many elements appear on a typical Web page, examine the page in Figure 4.1.

Figure 4.1 Sample Web Page

The items in this page include

⭐ The logo type in a marketing treatment, a stylized graphic of a globe

⭐ The company name, in the official corporate font, prepared as a graphic image

☆ Five menu items across the top, each prepared as a graphic image

☆ A headline in a blue banner followed by a column of text items, some of them hyperlinks

☆ A photo of an airplane superimposed on a Web page

☆ A small animated globe in the lower right

☆ A "Flight Search" form along the left

☆ Seven buttons along the bottom, each a graphic

Each of these items was carefully prepared and saved as a separate file. The corporate design office used Adobe Illustrator to create the logo and supplied it to the Web designer in digital form. The Web designer created the site title and the six menu labels in Photoshop using the official corporate font. The text was provided by the client's public relations office and supplied to the Web designer as a word-processing document. The photo was scanned into Photoshop, combined with the other image, reduced, and compressed as a Joint Photographic Experts Group (JPEG) file (graphics formats are discussed later in the chapter). The animated globe was prepared using Photoshop and GifBuilder.

That may sound like quite a bit of work for a simple Web page. But unless this work is done carefully, the page will not achieve its objectives.

As you create the list of the items for each page in your site, you're working much like a chef who makes a list of the ingredients for a meal. Armed with your list, you go out in search of the various items, gather what you can, and create the rest from scratch, much as the chef gathers meats, vegetables, and spices at the market. Next, you prepare each element using the appropriate software tool—a word processor for text, an image-editing program for pictures, and so forth—just as the chef slices the vegetables in a food processor and sears the meat in a heavy skillet.

Like a chef, you must pay special attention to the preparation of the elements because the final product is only as good as its parts. This chapter guides you in locating, editing, and saving each kind of material as you develop a solid Web site.

◎◎ Preparing the Elements: Text

For most Web pages, the chief source of content is text. As you've learned, the style and display of text is important in making the user's experience comfortable and fulfilling. This section explains where to find text, how to prepare it, and how to save it so that it is easily imported into your Web page.

Sources for Text

The Web designer is seldom expected to compose text. Just as Ernest Hemingway's publishers did not expect him to set the type and run the press for *The Old Man and the Sea*, most organizations do not want Web designers to write the text for the Web sites they program. The text, often called **copy**, is usually provided by writers in an organization's public relations or corporate communication department. But you must know how to treat the text you receive and perhaps will need to advise the writers on the kind of text that works best on Web pages.

Often, the text is taken from available documents such as brochures, flyers, annual reports, business plans, and press releases. You should request that such text be delivered not in print but in **electronic form**, most often as a word-processing file. The best format is a Word document, or `.doc` file, from which it is easy to extract the text as a plain text (`.txt`) file. Many documents published by large organizations are created in desktop publishing programs such as Quark Xpress and delivered in the proprietary formats of those programs. That can be a problem if you don't own the program. Another popular document format is Portable Document Format (PDF). PDF files must be displayed with Adobe Acrobat Reader. Even though this software is free and ubiquitous, it's difficult to extract the text from a PDF file.

☆**TIP**   **Filename Extensions**

Filename extensions are three- or four-letter suffixes attached to filenames, such as `design.html` or `letter.doc` or `picture.jpg`. Computer operating systems and Web browsers use these filename extensions to determine the kind of file it is. The `.doc` extension indicates a Microsoft Word document; `.jpg` indicates an image file (in this case, a JPEG file). If a file has the wrong extension, the item will not be displayed. As you learn to prepare each kind of item, you'll learn the correct filename extensions to use.

If the text is delivered to you as a printed document, you must either

☆ Scan the page using an optical character recognition (OCR) software program such as OmniPage or TextBridge. OCR programs work with flatbed scanners to automatically convert printed text into a digital text file.

☆ Retype the text using a word processor. For short selections, this may be more efficient than scanning.

You might also use text from existing Web pages. To capture this text, open the Web page with your browser. If you need all or most of the text, the best method is to click Save As from the browser's File menu and then save the document as a plain text (`.txt`) file.

If you need only a paragraph or two, the following may be more efficient:

1. Select the text by pressing and dragging with the mouse.

2. Click Copy from the Edit menu.

3. Open a word-processing document.

4. Click Paste from the Edit menu.

5. Save the document in plain text format (`.txt`).

In addition to the sources already discussed, you can write the text from scratch. In many organizations, the quickest way to get the paragraph you need is to track

☆**WARNING** If you did not compose and write the text yourself, it probably belongs to someone else. You should ask the author for permission to publish the text on your Web site. Even if the original page has no copyright notice, the author retains the right to control the distribution of the writing. A later section in this chapter covers copyright in more depth. At this point, realize that most materials published in print or on the Web belong to their authors and cannot be used on your site without permission.

down the person responsible for that topic and then interview him in person or over the telephone. Type his answers into your word processor, edit it for good style, and then have the interviewee review it to make sure you got it right.

Tools for Editing Text

No matter how you acquire text, it will need editing. Existing documents are often too long, or written in the wrong style, for effective communication on a Web page. Text sections may need added features such as subheads and bulleted lists. Moreover, text copied from existing Web pages is often sprinkled with carriage returns, tabs, indents, and other characters that need to be stripped out.

The best tool for editing is a word processor such as Microsoft Word. You should open each text item, no matter what its source, in Word and look at it to make sure it's in proper form. Here are some things to look for as you edit:

☆ If you copied the text from a Web page, look for carriage returns at the end of each line. Remove them using the Replace item under the Edit menu. Replace each carriage return with a space.

☆ Remove any columns, tab characters, extra line spacing, indents, justification, and other features that cannot or should not be carried forward to a Web page. To do this quickly, use the Replace item under the Edit menu.

☆ Unless the titles and subtitles are formatted exactly as you want them, change them to plain text.

☆ Line width, justification, line spacing, margins, and text size will not translate from the word processor to the Web. Remove any of these features so that you can see the text in its plainest form.

☆ For now, leave bulleted and numbered lists as they are. In many cases you can carry these styles forward to the Web page if you desire. In HTML, bulleted lists are called **unordered lists**, and numbered lists are called **ordered lists**.

☆ Reduce any unusual formatting or styles to regular text, with as little formatting as possible.

☆ Check spelling and grammar. It's a lot easier to do this now than later.

Consider the style of the text, as discussed in the next section, and rewrite it as necessary to make it appropriate for the Web.

◎◎ Writing for the Web

A writing style that works well in print might not communicate effectively in a Web page. Compared with readers of magazines, books, or newspapers, readers at a Web site view your page in a very different context. They're probably sitting in an office at a desk, and they're distracted by other work, other people, noise, and movements. Many of them would rather be doing something else than looking at your Web site. In a low-resolution medium, they're reading words that arrived seemingly from nowhere and can disappear quickly. They expect your site to be faster, more convenient, and more interactive than printed or in-person communications. As a result, the text must fit their context, expectations, and needs.

When you write or edit text for the Web, keep these points in mind:

⭐ Keep it short: Because of your readers' context, their attention span for written material is short. Most articles written for printed media need to be shortened for efficient use on the Web. Ruthlessly remove redundant paragraphs, restricting the prose to what is essential to your audience.

⭐ Use the pyramid structure: This journalistic style summarizes the story in the first paragraph. Make sure that the introduction includes the who, what, when, where, why, and how of the topic. Readers on the Web want to know whether your article is the one they need, and this summary paragraph helps them figure that out quickly. Later paragraphs tell the story in more detail.

⭐ Use subheads: Unless you are Stephen King, readers do not expect to experience text on your Web site as an unbroken, continuous narrative. To help readers find information quickly, provide subheads throughout the text. Subheads should be short and sweet and indicate what's in the paragraphs that follow.

⭐ Use bullets: When you have a series of separate but parallel ideas or examples, arrange them in bullets, omitting transitional phrases or sentences. This makes it easier to see the points in relation to each other and conserves space and time. You're reading a bullet list right now.

⭐ Provide links to interesting asides: To help readers delve more deeply, provide hyperlinks to materials located elsewhere on the Web. These materials are relevant or interesting but not essential to your immediate purpose. Link to examples, illustrations, background material, original sources, corporate Web sites, and so on.

Not all the text on your site can be rewritten to follow these style suggestions. But most can be, and should be, if it is to be effective. Here's an example. Consider the following text.

> ⭐ **TIP   Hypertext Links**
>
> Hypertext links are the clickable words in a Web site. When users click on a hypertext word, they're taken to another Web site to get more information or to see an example. Hypertext capability distinguishes the Web from all other text media. You can't click the words in a book or newspaper to connect to additional information. As a result, hypertext makes the Web a unique communication experience for both readers and authors.

Four score and seven years ago, our fathers brought forth upon this continent a new nation: conceived in liberty, and dedicated to the proposition that all men are created equal. Now we are engaged in a great civil war, testing whether that nation, or any nation so conceived and so dedicated, can long endure. We are met on a great battlefield of that war. We have come to dedicate a portion of that field as a final resting place for those who here gave their lives that this nation might live. It is altogether fitting and proper that we should do this.

But, in a larger sense, we cannot dedicate, we cannot consecrate, we cannot hallow this ground. The brave men, living and dead, who struggled here have consecrated it, far above our poor power to add or detract. The world will little note, nor long remember, what we say here, but it can never forget what they did here.

It is for us the living, rather, to be dedicated here to the unfinished work which they who fought here have thus far so nobly advanced. It is rather for us to be here dedicated to the great task remaining before us, that from these honored dead we take increased devotion to that cause for which they gave the last full measure of devotion, that we here highly resolve that these dead shall not have died in vain, that this nation, under God, shall have a new birth of freedom; and that government of the people, by the people, for the people, shall not perish from this earth.

Now let's consider how this famous text might be presented to readers of a Web site.

Lincoln's Speech at Gettysburg

Summary of the speech: Our nation was founded on principles of liberty and equality that are now being tested in a great war, one of whose battles was fought here in Gettysburg. We're here to honor those who died and to dedicate ourselves to improving the nation.

Founded on liberty and equality

Four score and seven years ago, our fathers brought forth upon this continent a new nation:

- *conceived in liberty, and*
- *dedicated to the proposition that all men are created equal.*

Civil War

Now we are engaged in a great civil war, testing whether that nation, or any nation so conceived and so dedicated, can long endure. We are met on a great battlefield of that war. We have come to dedicate a portion of that field as a final resting place for those who here gave their lives that this nation might live. It is altogether fitting and proper that we should do this.

Brave men

But, in a larger sense, we cannot dedicate, we cannot consecrate, we cannot hallow this ground. The brave men, living and dead, who struggled here have consecrated it, far above our poor power to add or detract. The world will little note, nor long remember, what we say here, but it can never forget what they did here.

Our task

It is for us the living, rather, to be dedicated here to the unfinished work which they who fought here have thus far so nobly advanced. It is rather for us to be here dedicated to the great task remaining before us, that from these honored dead we take increased devotion to that cause for which they gave the last full measure of devotion, that we here highly resolve that these dead shall not have died in vain, that this nation, under God, shall have a new birth of freedom; and that government

- *of the people,*
- *by the people,*
- *for the people,*

shall not perish from this earth.

This text example was already quite short, so its length was not changed. But the editor added a title, several subtitles, and a summary, presented certain key ideas with bullets, and added hypertext links. (Lincoln's words were designed to be listened to, not to be read, and they may not profit from the editing they endured in this example. But if this speech were presented on a Web site, such modifications might make it easier to read and understand.)

Saving Text Files

After you've edited the text, you need to save it in an appropriate format. If you're using a word processor such as Microsoft Word, you have two choices: to save the file as a plain text (`.txt`) file or as Hypertext Markup Language (HTML). An article having no titles, formatting, bullets, or lists should be saved as a plain text file. An article with formatting that you want to preserve on the Web page can be saved in HTML format.

★ To save as a text file: In Word, click Save As from the File menu, and then click Text Only from the Save As Type drop-down menu. This saves the text with no formatting, in a form easily imported into most Web page editing programs. Word automatically adds the filename extension `.txt`.

To save in HTML: Word and many other word processors can save the text document in HTML format, ready to be read by a browser or pasted into a Web page. Saving the file as HTML will preserve simple formatting such as font size, styles, bullets, and numbered lists. It will also preserve any hypertext links that you created in Word. However, this method may not save the text exactly as you intended.

☆TIP   Organizing Your Files

As you save your files, it's a good idea to organize them in a place where they will easily be found. Before saving this first text file, create a new folder with a simple, single-word name. As you gather the elements of your Web site, save them all in this folder.

☆DO IT YOURSELF   Prepare Text

Now is the time to gather and prepare the text for your Web site. This may take some time, especially if you need to write the copy from scratch or edit it heavily. Look at the spec sheet you prepared for your flow chart (see Chapter One). For every page that calls for text, make sure you have prepared and saved it properly. To help you find these text files later, note each of the filenames on the spec sheet.

◎◎ Preparing the Elements: Numbers

Most numbers in Web sites are simply part of the text and need no special treatment. Here's an example: "The XYZ Corporation today reported a net income for the third quarter of 56 cents per share." You can gather, prepare, and edit such statistics in a word processor along with the rest of the text. Conventionally, the whole numbers one through nine are spelled out, and larger numbers such as 14 or 567 are represented with numerals. For ease of reading, use commas in numerals having more than four digits (for example, 10,567).

When numbers are displayed on a Web site in tables or graphs, they need special preparation. You usually receive such numbers in a spreadsheet, but they may also arrive in a database or on paper.

The page illustrated in Figure 4.2 shows a table of numbers with many rows and columns, and Figure 4.3 shows a graph derived from a series of **values** and **labels**. The labels are the words that describe the categories of numbers; the values are the numbers themselves. Most numerical tables and graphs contain both labels and values.

Regardless of the source of the numbers, most Web designers prepare numerical information in a spreadsheet, where they edit it into proper form and develop any needed graphics. From the spreadsheet the numerical information is saved in a special tab-delimited form and later imported into the Web page. Table 4.1 summarizes the various sources of numerical information.

Preparing the Elements: Numbers

Table 1: Numbers of deaths and death rates

Back　Forward　Stop　Refresh　Home　AutoFill　Print　Mail

Address: http://www.nt.who.int/whosis/statistics/whsa/whsa_table1_process.cfm?path=statistics,whsa,whsa_table1,endpoint&language=english

Argentina 1994

Demographic data...

ICD-9 BTL codes	Cause groupings	Sex	Number of deaths at ages (in years) and by sex, and Age-sex-specific death rates per 100 000 population (infant death rates are per 100 000 live births)											
			All ages	< 1	1-4	5-14	15-24	25-34	35-44	45-54	55-64	65-74	75+	Age not specified
-	All causes	M	141 657	8 393	1 217	1 295	3 863	4 318	6 463	12 556	23 437	34 305	44 862	948
		F	112 326	6 342	973	808	1 573	2 010	3 783	6 482	11 584	21 758	56 401	612
		M	841.4	2415.6	87.6	38.5	127.6	182.3	312.2	756.5	1817.8	3798.2	10603.2	
		F	642.5	1943.4	72.3	24.8	52.9	84.8	175.7	374.1	802.4	1885.8	7836.7	
01-07, 184	Infectious and parasitic diseases	M	4 690	454	132	54	94	150	226	397	682	1 021	1 451	29
		F	4 041	329	114	51	64	110	162	252	381	735	1 823	20
		M	27.9	130.7	9.5	1.6	3.1	6.3	10.9	23.9	52.9	113.0	342.9	
		F	23.1	100.8	8.5	1.6	2.2	4.6	7.5	14.5	26.4	63.7	253.3	
011	Typhoid fever	M	-	-	-	-	-	-	-	-	-	-	-	
		F	-	-	-	-	-	-	-	-	-	-	-	
		M	-	-	-	-	-	-	-	-	-	-	-	
		F	-	-	-	-	-	-	-	-	-	-	-	
010, 019, 012-016	Other intestinal infectious diseases	M	339	167	45	8	1	2	4	7	18	33	52	2
		F	276	118	37	5	1	1	4	8	10	24	67	1
		M	2.0	48.1	3.2	0.2	0.0	0.1	0.2	0.4	1.4	3.7	12.3	
		F	1.6	36.2	2.7	0.2	0.0	0.0	0.2	0.5	0.7	2.1	9.3	
020-021	Tuberculosis of respiratory	M	651	5	9	6	20	51	75	94	121	142	127	1

Internet zone

Figure 4.2 Web Page with Table of Numbers

Figure 4.3 Web Page with Graph

Table 4.1 Working with Numbers

Source	Treatment
Created from scratch	Enter the labels and numbers into a spreadsheet such as Microsoft Excel.
Printed materials	Enter the labels and numbers into a spreadsheet such as Microsoft Excel.
A database file	Export the database file in tab-delimited form, and then import it into a spreadsheet such as Microsoft Excel.
A text file	Export the text file in tab-delimited form, and then import it into a spreadsheet such as Microsoft Excel.
A spreadsheet	Open the spreadsheet in a program such as Microsoft Excel.

Tools for Editing Numbers

A spreadsheet program such as Microsoft Excel provides tools both for organizing the numbers into a table and for creating charts and graphs. Here are the basic steps for using Excel to prepare numerical information:

1. Import the data from a text, database, or spreadsheet file, or enter it from the keyboard. Data to be imported should be in tab-delimited or comma-delimited form. To import the files, click Open from Excel's File menu.

2. Use mathematical formulas and functions to derive totals, averages, and other necessary data. Available functions can be viewed under Excel's Insert menu.

3. Edit and format the spreadsheet for optimal display of information. Keep labels short, preferably a single word. Eliminate blank rows and columns. But don't tinker with text styles or alignment in the spreadsheet; they will not come across when the file is imported into the Web page.

4. Save the spreadsheet as a tab-delimited text file. Click Save As from the File menu, and then click Text (Tab Delimited) from the pop-up menu. Use a file-name that you will remember, and make a note of it on your spec sheet.

Working with Spreadsheets

All spreadsheets have certain functions in common. Here are a few of the most popular.

☆ To enter a formula: Place the pointer in the cell where you want the results of the calculation to appear. Type an equal sign (=), and then type your formula. Or click Function from the Insert menu, choose from a list of formulas, and then complete the formula.

☆ To sum a column of numbers: Select the cell below the bottom of the column. Type =SUM(, and then select the column, from its top cell to its bottom cell, by pressing and dragging the mouse. Then type). Your formula should look like this: =SUM(A1:A5). To see the results, press the Return key.

☆ To copy a formula across several columns: Select the cell containing the formula, and then press the mouse button and drag to select the cells you want to copy it to. When they are selected, click Fill...Right or Fill...Down from the Edit menu. This will fill in the selected cells with the formula from the first cell.

☆ To make a graph: To select the rows and columns you want to use in your graph, press the mouse button and drag. Under the Insert menu, click Chart. Then click on the type of graph you want and click Finish.

☆ To modify the format of a graph: Select the graph. Then use the items under the Chart menu to modify various aspects of the graph.

Displaying Numbers on the Web

You can display numerical data in tables, graphs, charts, or a combination. Tables are best for items that need to be referenced and looked up individually. Graphs or charts are better for showing trends over time or comparative distributions. To display a list of products, dimensions, and prices, for example, a simple table with labels and numbers may suffice. For a record of high and low temperatures over time, you might use a graph so that the trend is clear.

You can import data saved from a spreadsheet directly into a table in most Web-page editing programs. But first make sure that the table will fit the limited display space. A good test is to shrink the spreadsheet window to the space available on your Web page, perhaps 500 pixels. That's three-fifths of the distance across an 800 by 600 pixel display, and halfway across a 1024 by 768 pixel display. If you cannot see the entire table without scrolling across, you can be sure the table will not fit into your Web page.

If you develop graphs in a spreadsheet program, you must save them as image files and then include them as images in the Web page. To use Excel to prepare the graph, follow these steps:

1. Determine the type of graph best suited to your data. Use a **column graph** to compare the measurements of discrete items, such as the heights of basketball players. Use a **line** or **area graph** to compare a continuous measurement over time, such as temperature or stock price. Use a **pie graph** (also known as a **pie chart**) to display parts that make up a whole, such as the categories of a budget.

2. Determine the space available on the Web page for the graph. A glance at your design sketch, and a careful measurement of pixels, should help you figure this out. A common size is 320 pixels wide by 240 pixels high.

3. Create the graph from the data in the spreadsheet. Modify the graph until it shows the key trends clearly and simply. Add a title. Adjust the size of the graph to meet the exact specifications of the Web page.

4. Select the graph. You will know it is selected when you see the eight little black squares, called **handles**, around the edge of the graph. With the graph selected, click Copy from the Edit menu.

5. Open Adobe Photoshop or another image-editing program. Click New from the File menu to create a new document window. Click Paste from the Edit menu to paste the image copied from Excel into this new window.

6. Using the Mode menu, convert this image to Index color. Save it as a `.gif` (Graphics Interchange Format) file. Give this file a Web-legal filename, and save it where you can easily locate it later.

⭐**WARNING**   Only certain filenames work universally across the World Wide Web. If you use an illegal filename, users won't be able to see the file. Filenames should contain only letters and numbers—no spaces, no unusual punctuation, no special characters, no capital letters, no brackets, no colons. All filenames must end with an identifying extension. Use `.htm` or `.html` for Web pages; use `.jpg` for JPEG image files; use `.gif` for GIF image files. Use `.mov` for QuickTime movie files, and `.aif` for sound files in the Audio Interchange Format.

⭐**SHORTCUT**   You don't have to use a spreadsheet to create a table. If you're creating a small table with fewer than a dozen numbers and no totals, averages, or graphics, you can easily create it from the keyboard directly into the Web-page editing program as you're assembling the page.

◎ Preparing the Elements: Images

Most Web pages contain images. They vary from a small company logo that appears in one corner to a banner ad that appears at the top of the page to a news photo in the middle to the menu bar that spans the bottom of the page. Each of these images must be gathered or created and then prepared and saved as a separate file. A typical commercial Web page might include 50 or 60 image files!

Where do these images come from? How are they created and edited? How should they be saved in the proper format for use on a Web page?

Like the ingredients for a meal, images come in many forms, and not all of them come from the same place. The master chef in a gourmet restaurant selects her beef at the best butcher shop in town and then travels to the greengrocer for the freshest vegetables and to the bakery for the perfect loaf of bread to accompany the feast. She may also stop at the dairy for milk and eggs and at the winery for the proper vintage. An experienced chef understands the need for gathering the best ingredients from a variety of sources.

Similarly, you must become the master of images, knowing what source to use for the kinds of pictures you need. You also must know how to work with the images to get them into the best form for display on a Web page.

Sources for Images

The sponsor of your site may provide all the images, but this is not the usual situation. Even those images you receive from the sponsor will need to be edited so that they work well on the Web page. More typically, you must gather images from variety of sources:

★ A company logo prepared in Adobe Illustrator and saved in Encapsulated PostScript (EPS) format, delivered on a floppy disk

★ A photograph of the company president on 8×10 glossy photo paper

★ A pencil sketch of a technical diagram

★ An illustration to be copied from an existing company Web site

★ A series of pictures in a paper copy of the company's internal magazine

★ A videotape taken at last year's company picnic, from which you need to extract some pictures of happy employees

★ A photo of the company headquarters on a sunny day

★ A specification to obtain "a photo of a beautiful sunset with a sailboat in the background"

★ A call for a faded background image of the company logo "that looks like a watermark" and will appear behind the text on certain pages

Preparing each of these images calls for its own set of tools and techniques. You can scan some of them using a flatbed scanner. Others might be taken on location with a digital camera, and still others will need to be drawn from scratch. A few can be downloaded from other Web sites or gathered from a CD-ROM image collection. Most of them will require editing in a program such as Adobe Photoshop. All of them will need to be saved in a size and format suitable for display on the Web pages where they belong.

Scanning

You can use a flatbed scanner to digitize photographs, sketches, illustrations from books and magazines, even small objects—anything that will fit on the glass of the scanner. Scanners are made by various manufacturers and use a variety of software controls, but all of them work in about the same way.

★**WARNING** Like text, most images are copyrighted. You must get the owner's permission to use them on your site. An exception is **clip art**, which in many cases can be used freely without permission.

★**TIP**   **Digitization**

Digitization is the process of turning an image into a file that can be manipulated and stored on a computer. The image is divided into thousands of tiny squares or dots, each one numbered to reflect its color. The scanner or digital camera sends the numbers to the computer, where the image is displayed. Although the digitized image may look like the original photo, a close look reveals the dots.

Many scanners work with image-editing software such as Photoshop to acquire and display the images. The scanner software is often included as a plug-in or TWAIN resource. TWAIN stands for Technology Without an Interesting Name, and like a plug-in provdes an interface between the image-ediitng software and the scanner. To use the scanner, you connect it to the computer and then open Photoshop. Click Import from the File menu, and then choose the scanner's plug-in from the list. The scanner's control window will appear.

In the scanner control window, you set the parameters for the scan and then conduct the scan. For most images, you should set the resolution to 72 dots per inch, the resolution of the computer screen. You should use a higher resolution only if the object to be scanned is very small and will be displayed larger than life size on the Web page.

Place the item on the scanner, and close the cover so that the item is as flat as possible on the glass. Click the Preview or Prescan button. The scanner will take several seconds to create a low-resolution overview of the item and display it in the scanner control window. When this preview is complete, you can stretch or shrink the selection as necessary to scan only the part of the image that you need. Then click the Scan or Final button. Be patient as the scanner does its work. When it's finished, you will see a new Photoshop window containing the image at the resolution you set. Now you can use Photoshop tools to edit, adjust, and then save the image.

Using a Digital Still Camera

A digital camera captures what it sees onto a storage device—a floppy disk, a memory stick, or memory chips inside the camera. Instead of film, the camera contains a light-sensitive plate that's divided into thousands of tiny dots. The camera's lens focuses the image onto the plate. When you snap the picture, the data from the plate—a series of numbers representing the colors focused on each dot—is sent to the storage device, where it is saved.

When you've filled the camera with images, you take the storage device or the camera itself to your computer to transfer the images.

To gather images for a Web page, first make sure the camera's batteries are well charged. Now you're ready to compose the picture. On the Web, pictures are smaller and of lower resolution than those in a magazine or a book. Follow these suggestions to produce good pictures for your Web page:

☆ Light: A brightly lit subject will photograph better than one cloaked in shadows. Position the source of light behind the camera. Arrange the subject so that the light shines on him at an angle and not directly. This keeps people from squinting and provides pleasant shadows to show off texture and detail.

☆ Tight: Let your subject fill the frame. In a group shot, crowd the people close together. Avoid groups of more than five. Include only heads and shoulders in the photo. For buildings or rooms, you don't need to include the entirety; often, a close shot of one interesting element looks better.

Preparing the Elements: Images

☆ Sight: The camera sees not only your subject but also the background. Shoot pictures against a plain background (but keep people three feet away from a wall). Remove distracting items before shooting.

☆ Write: Words do not show up well in photos, especially on the Web. Use photos for people, buildings, and events. Use text elements for words. The nice letters you see on the bulletin board may be readable through the lens of the camera, but they will be indecipherable on-screen.

☆ Uptight: People seem more alive when they're not posing. If you're photographing two people, ask them to talk or look at an item rather than stare into the camera. Getting them to do something will help them relax and make a more "human" photograph. Photograph people actually doing their work rather than standing in a pose.

Each model of digital camera uses its own method to get the images into the computer. Some of them connect with a cable and use special software to transfer the file. Others store the images in JPEG format on a floppy disk, from which they can be copied to the computer. No matter how the images come across, you use image-editing software such as Photoshop to open, edit, and format them for inclusion in your Web page.

Getting Images from the Web

Some of the images you need may already exist on the Internet, perhaps in the client's existing site. Such images are already in proper Web format and can be used without modification. The client may supply these images in GIF or JPEG format. You can also use your Web browser to easily capture these images.

☆ **WARNING** In most situations, you need permission of the owner of the Web site in order to use an image.

To capture an image from a Web site, follow these steps:

1. Position the pointer over the picture you want to capture. On Windows, right-click the mouse, and you will see a pop-up menu. On Macintosh, press the mouse button until you see the pop-up menu.

2. Click Save Image to Disk (Netscape), Download Image to Disk (Explorer on Macintosh), or Save Picture to Disk (Explorer on Windows).

3. Save the image file to your Web site folder. Do not change the file extension.

☆ **TIP**   Organizing Your Files

A large Web site with hundreds of pages should be organized into several folders (or directories) and subfolders (or subdirectories). Even if your site isn't very large, you should organize your folders carefully. Create one folder for the site itself, and give it a Web-legal, one-word filename, with no spaces or punctuation. Within this folder create three subfolders named *images*, *video*, and *sound*. As you gather the elements for your Web site, save them in these folders.

> ⭐ **WARNING** Images that you capture from a Web site usually cannot be enlarged without pixelation. Pixelation means that the pixels get so big you can easily see each one with the unaided eye. So if you're looking for an image of a screen-filling yacht, don't capture a thumbnail-size picture of a dinghy from a Web site. You can, however, shrink images from Web pages quite easily.

Using a CD-ROM Image Collection or Clip Art

Many publishers provide CD-ROMs containing thousands of images suitable for Web sites. Many of these images are "royalty-free," meaning that the publisher grants you permission to use them however you wish. Most of these CD-ROMs include a search engine so that you can find an image by entering key words or even key colors. When you have found the image you need, save it to your *images* folder.

These images come in various file formats and resolutions. For use on a Web site, choose the GIF or JPEG format at a resolution of 72 dots (or pixels) per inch.

Capturing a Still Image from Video

Sometimes the image you need is contained in a video. If your computer is equipped with a video input device, you can capture a still image from the video. Many newer computers, such as the iMac and iBook from Apple Computer, include FireWire ports, to which you can connect a digital video (DV) camcorder. To capture a still image, you connect the camcorder, play the tape, and then use the video-editing software (on the iMac it's called iMovie) to capture the image you need.

Usually, images captured from video are not ready to be posted directly to a Web site. You need to resize and edit them in a program such as Photoshop and then save them in JPEG or GIF format.

> ⭐ **WARNING** In most situations, you need permission of the owner of the video in order to use a still image on a Web site.

Tools for Editing Images

When you've gathered your images, the next task is to edit them to the proper size and quality and to save them in a proper format. No matter where you acquired the image, it's a good idea to open it in an image-editing program such as Adobe Photoshop, making sure it meets the demands of your design. With the image open, ask yourself these key questions:

⭐ Is it the right size?

⭐ Is the resolution correct?

⭐ Is it closely cropped so that the subject fills the space?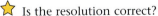

⭐ Is it bright and clear enough?

⭐ Are the colors true?

⭐ Does the content of the image fit the specs of the Web site plan?

Opening the Image

You can't simply double-click an image file and expect it to open in Photoshop or another image-editing program. The proper method is to open Photoshop and then click Open from Photoshop's File menu. Photoshop can open almost every kind of image, but it may have trouble opening certain types of files, including

★ Files created in Adobe Illustrator and saved in Illustrator's proprietary format. To solve this problem, open the image in Illustrator and save it in EPS format, which Photoshop can open.

★ Animations created with Macromedia Flash and similar programs. To capture a single frame from such an animation, make a screen capture, save it, and open it with Photoshop.

Photoshop and similar image-editing programs open the image in a new window and present a tool palette, such as the one shown in Figure 4.4. Pausing the pointer over each tool will display its name.

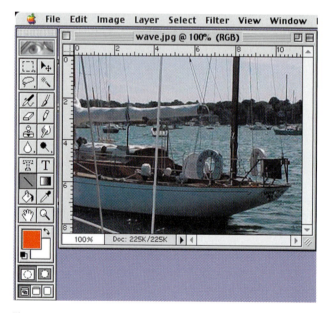

Figure 4.4 Image-Editing Window and Tool Palette

Editing the Image

You use the tools to select parts of the image, to draw on it, to erase or copy parts of it, and to select colors. You use the menus to adjust, resize, modify, filter, distort, and apply special effects to the image. This book cannot include a complete course in Photoshop, but many volumes are available that can teach you how to edit images with this powerful program. In Addison-Wesley's Web Wizard series, *The*

Web Wizard's Guide to Multimedia, by James Lengel, provides much more detail on preparing images for a Web site.

Here, you'll learn about the basic image-editing operations that often confront Web designers. Following is a summary of selected items from Photoshop's tool palette:

⭐ Marquee tool: Use it to select rectangular or circular parts of the image. To adjust the size and shape of the area selected by the tool, double-click it.

⭐ Lasso tool: Selects odd-shaped portions of the image. Press and drag around the portion you want to select.

⭐ Magic wand: Selects an area having a color similar to the spot where you click. The tolerance of the similarity is adjustable.

⭐ Move tool: Press and drag to move selected parts of the image.

⭐ Zoom tool: If you click on the image, it zooms in. If you press and hold the Option key as you click, it zooms out.

⭐ Paint bucket: Pours foreground-color paint into the image.

⭐ Eyedropper: Picks up a color from the image at the spot where it's clicked and puts it into the foreground paint chip.

⭐ Pencil: Draws like a pencil (in the foreground color).

⭐ Paintbrush: Paints like a brush (in the foreground color).

⭐ Smudge tool: As you press and drag the mouse, it smudges the image under the tool.

⭐ Eraser: Replaces areas where you press and drag the mouse with the background color.

⭐ Airbrush: Works like a paintbrush but with a softer edge.

⭐ Toning Tool: Softly lightens the image wherever you drag it.

⭐ Blur tool: Blurs the part of the image you drag it over.

⭐ Rubber stamp: Copies a portion of the image. Option-click to pick up an area of the image. Then click and drag to paint that area somewhere else.

⭐ Foreground paint chip: Specifies the color that will be painted by the pencil, paintbrush, airbrush, or text tool.

⭐ Background paint chip: Specifies the color that will be left after you use the eraser.

⭐ Line tool: Draws a straight line. Press and hold the Shift key to draw horizontal, vertical, and 45-degree diagonal lines.

To be used on a Web site, many images will need simple editing. Here are some hints for improving images:

⭐ Crop the image: Images work best on the Web if they are closely cropped so that the subject takes up most of the rectangle. To crop an image, click and drag the marquee tool to outline the rectangle that you want to crop to. Then click Crop from the Image menu.

★ Lighten the image: Click Adjust from the Image menu, and then click Brightness and Contrast. Adjust the brightness and contrast sliders until you achieve the effect you desire. The same method is used to darken an image.

★ Apply a special effect: Click one of the items under the Filter menu, and apply it to the picture. Don't be afraid to experiment—you can always undo any effect that you create. Useful effects for Web images are Sharpen, Noise, Blur, and Stylize.

★ Adjust the colors: If the color seems off, try using the Color Balance and Hue/Saturation tools that are found in the Adjust item under Photoshop's Image menu.

★ Stretch or shrink: Before trying this, make sure you are viewing the image at 100% of its size. Look in the title bar to make sure it reads 100%. Click Zoom In or Zoom Out under the View menu to adjust the view. To enlarge an image, click Image Size under the Image menu, and then enter the new size in the dialog box that appears. But remember that if you stretch an image too far, it will lose definition and become pixelated.

Drawing an Image from Scratch

You can use Photoshop to create a simple image, diagram, or logo from scratch. To begin, click New from the File menu, and create a document window in the exact pixel size called for in your site's specification. Set the resolution of the document at 72 pixels per inch. Then use the drawing tools—the pencil, the paintbrush, the line tool, and the text tool—to draw the image. These tools use the color selected in the foreground paint chip.

To create a gradient background, one that blends gradually from one color to another across the screen, choose a foreground and background color in the color chips. Select the gradient tool, and then press and drag across the window in the direction you want the gradient to appear. Dragging from left to right will create a gradient from the foreground color to the background color horizontally across the window. To create a diagonal gradient, click and drag the tool from one corner to its opposite.

Setting Size and Resolution

You should edit your images to the size predetermined in your site design. The specifications should include the size of the image in pixels, such as "a 320 by 240-pixel picture of the CEO pointing to the new XYZ-mobile." Before saving the edited image, make sure that its size is correct and that its resolution is 72 pixels per inch. To adjust these variables, click Image Size under the Image menu.

★ **TIP**   Setting a higher resolution will *not* increase the sharpness or definition of an image. These are limited by the resolution of the user's computer display. Setting a higher resolution will only increase the file size and thus the download time of the image. It will not look any better to viewers.

Setting Color Mode and Depth

If you are working with color photographs, you should set Photoshop to work in RGB ("red green blue") mode. These are the three colors used in the computer display. Each pixel is composed of red, green, and blue components. All other colors are created by combining these three colors in different proportions on the display. In Photoshop, you set the color mode under the Image menu.

For nonphotographic material, such as diagrams and logos, it's better to work in Index color mode. These types of images are best saved in Graphics Interchange Format (GIF) format, as described next, and that requires Index color mode. In this mode, the number of color combinations is limited. The resulting smaller files save space and download faster.

Saving Image Files: Compression and File Formats

After you've edited a file and adjusted the image to the proper size and resolution, you can save it in a format ready for use on the Web. Images can be saved in one of the compressed file formats such as GIF, JPEG, and Portable Network Graphics (PNG). GIF is best for nonphotographic images such as logos, diagrams, maps, and other pictures with lines and areas of solid color. JPEG is used for photographs and for images with complex colors that blend into one another gradually. PNG is a new **lossless** compression scheme that's just beginning to be used.

GIF and JPEG and PNG images are **compressed**. This means that their files do not contain full information on color and brightness for every single pixel in the image. It also means that the files are much smaller than they would be in an uncompressed format. Smaller files download faster and display faster on the user's computer. An uncompressed 320 by 240-pixel photograph would occupy 225,000 bytes. That's because each of its 76,800 pixels requires 24 bits to store its color information, for a total of 1,843,200 bits of data (one byte equals eight bits). Sending all these data over a 56K modem (that's 56,000 bits per second, more or less) would take about 33 seconds. Very few viewers are willing to wait that long for a single small image to appear.

Compressing a typical 320 by 240-pixel image using the JPEG algorithm would reduce its file size to about 27,000 bytes, about one-tenth the original size. The compressed image would download to the modem user in about three seconds, and the effects of the compression would hardly be noticeable.

A complete discussion of compression algorithms and effects is beyond the scope of this book. Further discussion can be found in *The Web Wizard's Guide to Multimedia,* also in Addison-Wesley's Web Wizard series. At this stage, it's sufficient to understand that you should usually use GIF compression for diagrams, and JPEG for photographs.

When you're saving a file in Photoshop, click Save As from the File menu. This gives you a choice of compression methods and file formats. If you click JPEG, you'll be presented another choice: the extent of compression. The more compression, the smaller the file size but the lower the visual quality of the image. For images that are key to the success of your Web site, you should experiment a bit, saving them at different levels of compression to see which one results in the best trade-off of file size and quality.

Photoshop can save images in a variety of formats, but JPEG, GIF, and PNG are the only choices for most Web pages.

Note: If you are using version 5 or older of Photoshop, you may find that you can't save in GIF format if you're working in RGB color mode, and you can't save in JPEG if you're working in Index color mode. And you can't save in either format if the image contains separate layers. So, if Photoshop limits your file format choices when you use Save As, as illustrated in Figure 4.5, check to see that you're in the right color mode and that you have flattened the image to combine the separate layers. You'll find Mode under the Image menu, and Flatten under the Layers menu. The latest versions of Photoshop include an option called Save for Web, which takes care of these problems.

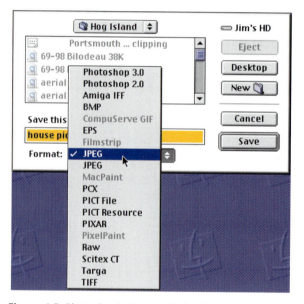

Figure 4.5 Photoshop's Save As Dialog Box

Ownership, Permission, and Copyright Issues

You must identify the authorship of every element that you prepare for your Web site. No one can publish on the Web text, images, animations, sound, or video that belong to someone else unless she has obtained permission to do so. Even if there is no copyright notice on an item that you scan, copy, or download, that does not mean you can use it without permission. The author of a work is considered to own the copyright automatically. No registration or notice is required.

It is not fair to use someone else's work on your Web site without asking permission and, if required, paying compensation. You would not want one of your hard-earned projects to be used on someone else's site without your permission.

Neither the United States nor local authorities employs copyright police who search the Web looking for violations of the copyright laws. But many of the authors and copyright owners do. They consider their words, images, songs, and video to be their property, and they consider people who publish them without permission to be thieves. Copyright law allows owners of a work to seek damages and penalties in court for any unauthorized use of their property.

Some exceptions exist. A student in a classroom developing a Web site as part of a class assignment that is seen only by the teacher and classmates may use copyrighted materials without seeking permission. A journalist may quote from a book as part of a Web review without getting permission from the author. These are considered "fair use" of copyright materials and are explicitly allowed by U.S. copyright law. Also, works in the public domain, such as the Declaration of Independence or the Gettysburg Address, cannot be copyrighted and may be used on a Web site fairly and legally.

The United States Copyright Office at `http://lcweb.loc.gov/copyright` provides more details that can help you figure out how to understand the use of materials.

Next Steps

The text, numbers, and images are ready, but what about the other elements? Chapter Five explains how to gather and prepare your site's multimedia elements: animation, sound, video, and interactive forms.

⭐ Summary

▶ Preparing the various elements of your site's content is the most critical part of the design process.

▶ You should write and edit text for the Web in a style that's consistent with the medium, and you should organize it so that it's easy to navigate.

▶ You can display numerical information on your Web page in the form of tables and graphs prepared in a spreadsheet such as Microsoft Excel.

▶ To achieve your site's objectives, you must prepare the images, carefully sourcing, cropping, sizing, editing, compressing, and saving them by using a program such as Adobe Photoshop.

▶ No matter what the source or style of the content, you must either compose it yourself or make sure that you have any needed permissions from its author.

⭐ Online References

Writing for the Web. A site with connections to many articles on writing text so that it communicates well on a Web page.
http://www.useit.com/papers/webwriting/

Creating Graphics for the Web. This fortnightly series of articles from England provides hints and tips on preparing images.
http://www.widearea.co.uk/designer/

⭐ Review Questions

1. How many separate content elements exist on a typical corporate Web page?

2. How should text for the Web be edited differently than text for a book or newspaper?

3. Explain how to use a spreadsheet to prepare tables and graphs for a Web page.

4. List three types of images that might be used on a Web page.

5. Trace the process of preparing a photograph to be used on a Web page.

6. Explain how an image is represented by a series of numbers.

7. List six image-editing tools included in a program such as Adobe Photoshop.

⭐ Hands-On Exercises

1. Connect to a corporate Web page, and download each of the separate elements onto your computer. Explain the purpose, the file format, and the method of preparation for each element.

2. Take an article from a magazine or newspaper, and edit and reformat it in Word to be suitable for publishing on a Web page. Save the page as HTML, and view the file with a Web browser.

3. Find a page on the Web whose text violates the principles set forth in this chapter. Then find a page that follows these guidelines. Compare the ways readers would respond to the text in the two pages.

4. Prepare a small table of numbers in a spreadsheet, and create a graph suitable for publishing on a Web page.

5. Use Photoshop to prepare an image for the Web. Resize it, crop it, lighten or darken it, and save it in both GIF and JPEG formats. View both versions with a Web browser and point out any visible differences.

CHAPTER FIVE

Gathering and Preparing Multimedia Elements

This chapter explains how to locate, gather, and prepare your site's multimedia elements, including animations, sound, video, and forms. It covers the software tools and file formats that work best for each type of element. Along the way, it deals with copyright issues, editing tools, sampling, compression, and databases.

◎◎ Chapter Objectives

- ⭐ To learn the techniques for acquiring, editing, and preparing animation files to be used on a Web page
- ⭐ To learn the techniques for acquiring, editing, and preparing sound files
- ⭐ To learn the techniques for acquiring, editing, and preparing video files
- ⭐ To understand how to prepare databases and other methods for handling user-supplied data from Web page forms

◎◎ Preparing the Elements: Animation

Animations are images that move. The simplest animations consist of several images displayed one after another in rapid succession, giving the impression of motion. Animations are commonly used in banner advertisements and sometimes are used to add explanations to diagrams. Although it's still rare, increasing numbers of Web sites include full-screen, television-like animation with moving titles and swirling shapes. Animation is an art, and instruction in the tools used to create complex, three-dimensional animations is beyond the scope of this book.

Once in a while, it might be a good idea to create an animation from scratch, but most Web designers rely on specialists for that purpose. Regardless of the source, a Web designer must know when and where to place an animation on the site.

> ☆**TIP**   **Do you really need animation?**
>
> Even though the viewer's eye is attracted to something that moves or blinks, most Web users become annoyed when distracted by animations that serve no purpose. Many Web sites do not need animation at all. Unless animation is necessary to the purposes of your site, you should not include it.

Sources for Animations

The best source for an animation depends on the purposes of your Web site. You can create a simple animation from scratch using Photoshop or an inexpensive animation program such as GifBuilder, GIF Construction Set, or Animation Shop. Many animated GIF files can be found on existing Web sites and in clip-art collections. You can order animations from a client's art department or commission them from professional digital animators.

> ☆**SHORTCUT**   **Easy Animations**
>
> You can create animations from short video clips or from certain photo sequences.

> ☆**WARNING**   Warning: Like a picture or a paragraph of text (see Chapter Four), an animation belongs to the person who created it. You cannot use it on your Web site without the permission of the owner.

Tools for Creating Animations

Table 5.1 shows some animation tools in approximate order of their power and complexity.

Table 5.1 Animation Tools

Software	Appropriate Use
Adobe Photoshop	The newest versions contain tools for creating and saving a series of images as an animated GIF. Each frame of the animation is created separately with standard Photoshop tools.
GifBuilder (Macintosh), GIF Construction Set (Windows)	These programs are used to build animated GIF files from an existing series of images.
Apple QuickTime Player	QuickTime Player Pro can be used to open a sequence of existing images, set the timing, and create an animation that can be saved as a QuickTime `.mov` file suitable for use on a Web page.
Macromedia Fireworks	This is a full-featured set of tools for creating animations and other images.
Macromedia Flash	Flash is designed for creating the large graphics animations that you see on many Web pages. It provides excellent tools and saves its files in the Shockwave-Flash (`.swf`) format.
Macromedia Director	The grandparent of Flash, this has been used for decades to create animations and interactive computer experiences. Its animation tools and interactive possibilities are unmatched, and its files are saved in Director (`.dcr`) format.
3-D rendering programs	These are used to create 3-D visualizations and the kind of animation seen in the movie *Toy Story*. They are expensive and have a steep learning curve, but they may be necessary to create certain technical or mechanical animations.

Each of these programs is unique, but they all work in the same manner. You follow these steps:

1. Import or draw the contents of the animation in the program.
2. Arrange the contents over time and space in a window or timeline.
3. Set parameters for speed, size, transitions, and resolution.
4. Preview and edit the results.
5. Save the animation in a form suitable for the Web.

Figure 5.1 shows a simple animation being created in Macromedia Director. On the right in the Score window is the timeline. The moving objects are displayed in the Stage window and again as members of the Internal Cast. Also shown is the Control Panel, which allows you to preview the work as you're creating it.

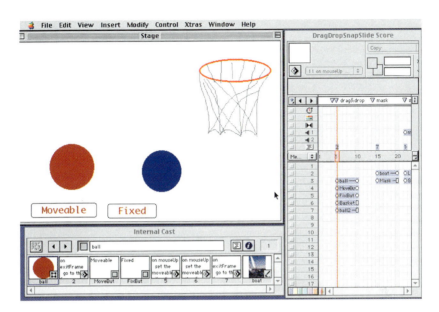

Figure 5.1 Macromedia Director Animation

Displaying Animation on the Web

Any of the animation file types described here can be embedded in the Web page or displayed in their own separate window (see Chapter Two). At this point, you should plan how the animation should appear. Most animations are embedded; when the page opens, the animation downloads and begins moving. For some animations, however, it may be better to display them in a separate window. This applies especially to those that are viewed over a span of Web pages or that need to be shown in their own window.

Most of the Web page editing programs that you will use to assemble your Web pages can easily import the kinds of animations described in this chapter. But not everyone in your audience will be able to see every animation, especially those that require a plug-in. Animations saved in GIF format need no plug-in; animations saved as QuickTime movies (`.mov`) require the QuickTime plug-in; and Flash (`.swf`) and Director (`.dcr`) animations require the Shockwave-Flash plug-in. Most new computers ship with these plug-ins already installed; otherwise, users must download the plug-in from its source. These plug-ins are free, but they require registration as well as knowledge and time to install.

The definition of your audience will determine how best to display animation on your site. To be sure that all users can view animations without worrying about plug-ins, an ultraconservative Web designer with an audience of computer novices will use only GIF animations. A considerate Web designer will tell the audience when a plug-in is necessary and will provide a link to the source. The designer of a

Web page aimed at a sophisticated audience of experienced computer users will not be afraid to take advantage of the latest animation techniques, relying on the viewers to install whatever plug-ins they need.

Saving Animation Files

As mentioned earlier, each animation-creation tool saves files in its own format. Some tools can also save the animation in formats that are not suitable for the Web. You must be careful to save your animation files in one of the formats that can be read by standard Web browsers. New animation file formats will be invented, and new plug-ins will become available, so the list in Table 5.1 does not exhaust all possibilities for all time. You must understand your audience well enough to determine when it is ready for the latest file format.

★**DO IT YOURSELF**   **Prepare Animations**

Prepare any animations called for in your Web site using some of the approaches described above. Save the files in proper format into your Web site folder.

◎◎ Preparing the Elements: Sound

Some of the Web pages in your site may call for sound, music, voice, or audio effects. You prepare each of these sounds as a separate file and save it on the Web server along with the HTML page files. To prepare these sound files, you must locate a source for the desired sound, use the appropriate sound-editing software, and save the file in one of the file formats suitable for the Web.

Sources for Sound

A few Web designers can sing, play a variety of musical instruments, and speak with a stentorian voice. They can record all the sounds they need directly into the computer's microphone. If you're not among those gifted individuals, you must locate the best source of the sounds called for in your site plan:

☆ For voices, the best approach is to record them directly into the sound-editing software on the computer. Usually, the narration or dialog is scripted by a writer and is read by the speaker into the computer's microphone in a sound-controlled environment. Although you can import voice from audiotape, you'll get better results with live recording. You can also obtain voices from compact discs, which provide much better quality than tape. Voice from a CD can be transferred directly to sound-editing software.

☆ It's difficult to record music well in the computer lab, so it's best to obtain it from a CD. Music is also available on the Internet as MP3 files, but most of these performances cannot be used on a Web site without permission of the owner. In addition, the sound quality may not be suitable for a professional Web site. You can also use Musical Instrument Digital Interface (MIDI) files, and they're the most efficient in terms of quality for a given file size. MIDI files are created with MIDI synthesizers and music sequencing software.

☆ You can record sound effects live at the computer or import them from CDs. Many publishers sell CDs containing hundreds of sound effects and musical clips that can be used royalty-free. Similar effects files can be downloaded from the Internet, edited, and used as long as permission is granted by the sound's creator or owner.

Tools for Editing Sound

Complete instruction on editing sound is beyond the scope of this book. More information is available in *The Web Wizard's Guide to Multimedia*. No matter what the source, you can import sounds into an editing program, where you can test, compress, and save them in a suitable format. Popular sound-editing software for Web work includes the following:

☆ Macromedia SoundEdit: This general-purpose, easy-to-use, multitrack program can import, export, and compress to and from most Web-capable file formats. Figure 5.2 shows three tracks in SoundEdit's document window as well as the Controls and Levels windows. The top track is a music clip; the middle track shows a voice-over; and the bottom track includes a sound effect at the conclusion.

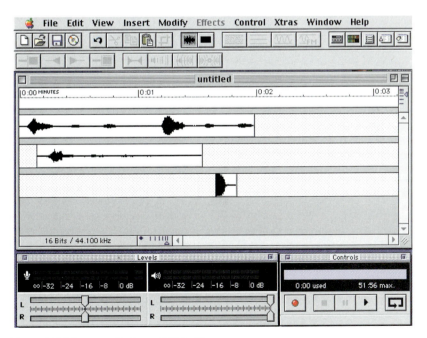

Figure 5.2 Macromedia SoundEdit In Use

Preparing the Elements: Sound

☆ SimpleSound (Macintosh) and RecordSound (Windows): You can use these sound-recording programs to record and save sounds but not for editing.

☆ SoundForge: Available only for Windows, this program lets you adjust many parameters but does not include multitrack editing.

☆ CoolEdit: Also Windows-only, this program provides simple recording and some mixing but no multitrack editing. CoolEdit Pro, at five times the price, has greater capabilities, including multitrack editing and support for many file formats.

These software tools use the computer's built-in microphone and audio input and output hardware. For more sophisticated sound recording and editing, you can buy specialized hardware and software such as that from Digidesign. Significantly more expensive, these tools are designed for professional recording studios.

All the tools work in the same way. First, you import the sound into the editing software through the microphone, from another device through audio inputs, or by direct transfer from a compact disc. Because CD sound is already in digital form, it need not be re-recorded by the computer. After you import the sound, you use the editor to adjust it as necessary—shortening it, changing its volume, adding effects, amplifying one track while attenuating another, and so forth. You then compress and save the file in a suitable format.

Sampling Rate

The sound you hear from a compact disc is **sampled** at a rate of 44 kilohertz. This means that a sample of sound was collected 44,000 times per second. Each sample contains 16 bits of information about the pitch and volume of the sound at that point in time. Like the numbers that represent the colors of each pixel in an image file, this sound information is recorded as a number, one number for each sample. This process of sampling is called **digitization**. Each track of a CD consists of a long series of numbers. When these numbers are converted back into sound and played very fast (44,000 numbers per second), they sound to your ear just like the original performance.

The problem is that each of the tracks contains a huge number of numbers. A typical track on a CD takes up 25MB. That's about 26 million bytes, or 210 million bits of information. To send one such uncompressed track through the World Wide Web over a 56K modem would take about an hour—longer than most users are willing to wait to hear the music on your Web page.

That's why you must compress the sound, reducing the file size as much as possible while at the same time maintaining as much sound quality as possible. Several methods have been developed to do this, and others are being invented as this book is written.

Saving Sound Files: Compression and File Formats

After you've edited a sound file, you use the sound-editing software to compress it. The compression method and file format you choose will be determined by the nature of your audience. Are they professional musicians who expect the highest-quality music and are willing to suffer long download times? Or are they novices for whom the quality of the voice narration is unimportant? Do most of your site visitors enjoy high-speed Internet connections, or are most of them likely to connect with modems requiring long download times? Are most of your users familiar with plug-ins? Do they understand how their browser handles files? The answers to these questions dictate your compression strategy and file format.

In addition to the file format, you must choose a **codec**: the algorithm used to compress the sound file. ("Codec" stands for compressor-decompressor.) Your compressed files must be decompressed by viewers. For instance, you might compress a music file using the Qdesign Music codec and saved in the QuickTime (`.mov`) format. A voice narration for another Web site might be compressed with the Qualcomm Purevoice codec and saved in the Audio Interchange File (`.aif`) format. Figure 5.3 shows a list of choices for saving and exporting sound files.

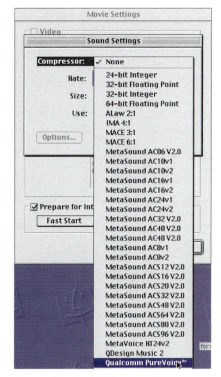

Figure 5.3 Typical Compression Algorithms for Sound Files

For a deeper discussion and explanation of compression and file formats for sound, see *The Web Wizard's Guide to Multimedia*.

Streaming Media

The sound clips described here exist as files on the Web server. From there, they are downloaded to the hard disk of the user's computer and then played. Because of the limitations of bandwidth, user patience, and disk space, these kinds of sounds are limited to short segments and small file sizes. In another method, **audio streaming**, the file never downloads to the user but instead plays immediately as it arrives. Audio streaming transmits a constant, real-time stream of sound to the user and also lets you use much larger files. Streaming requires a special server on the sender's side, and a plug-in on the receiver's side.

Three methods of audio streaming are popular on the Web: RealAudio, QuickTime Streaming, and Windows Media. The makers of these three technologies are in hot competition for market share and are constantly at work improving their products. RealAudio has the most users; QuickTime has the highest quality; and Windows Media is the newcomer. All three require a browser plug-in for users as well as special streaming software running on the Web server. To hear the latest examples of continuous streaming sound, you can visit the Web site of each sponsor:

★ RealAudio: `http://www.realaudio.com/`

★ QuickTime: `http://www.apple.com/quicktime/`

★ Windows media: `http://www.microsoft.com/windows/windowsmedia/`

Many radio stations broadcast 24 hours a day using streaming audio, and many Web sites use this technology to provide high-quality sound without time limitations.

No matter which file format and codes you choose, you must save the sound file in the right directory and use a Web-legal filename and extension. Sound files (except for streaming audio files) should be saved in the *sounds* subfolder you set up earlier inside the Web site folder. Save streaming files in a special streaming format on the streaming server.

★ **DO IT YOURSELF**   **Prepare Sound Files**

Use one or more of the approaches described above to prepare sound files for your Web site, and save them in proper form inside your Web folder.

◎◎ Preparing the Elements: Video

Not every Web site needs video to accomplish its purposes. But as computers become more like television in our lives, as Internet bandwidth increases, and as computers become more capable of decompressing and displaying video, Web visitors will increasingly expect video to be employed where appropriate. Of all the elements of a Web site, video is the most difficult and expensive to produce, prepare, and serve. But new software tools and new digital video (DV) cameras and connections make the preparation of video clips easier than ever before.

Sources for Video Material

Like sound, video can come from live sources, from existing videotapes, or from digital video files stored on CD-ROM or on Web sites:

★ Live sources: Shooting video with a DV camera is easy, and you can import DV output directly into a computer. When you're shooting a video clip for the Web, make sure the subject is well-lit, and use a tripod if possible. Zoom in for as tight a shot as possible, and keep the clips short and active. Avoid rapid pans and zooms. To record audio, use an external microphone placed near the speaker's mouth. The built-in microphone on most video camcorders will not give good results. Don't be afraid to take several versions of the same scene until you get one that works well. The same guidelines apply to video shot with an analog camcorder, but digitizing the analog video is much more difficult.

☆ Existing videotape: If you're using video material already recorded on tape, you can digitize it into the computer, edit it, and then save it in a suitable format. If your computer has an analog video input, connect the audio and video output of a video cassette player to the audio and video inputs of the computer, and then play the tape and import the video stream into your video-editing software. For a computer with DV (FireWire) input, you can convert the signal from analog to digital by using a DV camcorder between the video cassette player and the computer.

☆ CD-ROM sources: Video clips stored on optical media such as CD-ROM or DVD are already in digital form and compressed. You may need only import them into the video-editing program (to ensure that they are in a Web-ready format) and then save them to your video folder.

☆ Web sources: Video clips found on the Web are usually small and highly compressed and thus not of high quality. But they may, if they meet your needs, provide video suitable for your Web site. As with CD-ROM sources, you need permission from the owner of the video in order to use such a clip on your Web site.

☆**WARNING** The same requirements for permission apply to video files as to sound files.

Tools for Editing Video

Video is actually a series of still frames displayed rapidly on the computer screen to give the viewer the impression of continuous motion. Using video-editing software, you can adjust, modify, recombine, and apply effects to these frames and then compress and save the file in a format suitable for the Web. To use a video editor, follow these steps:

1. Import the video. Video from a DV camera is already in digital form and can be used directly in the video-editing software. Video from an analog camera must first be digitized, or captured, before it can be edited.

2. Adjust and edit the video (see Figure 5.4). Most video-editing programs let you cut, copy, paste, combine, and shorten video sequences as well as intersperse them with still images, music, and sound. Most of them provide tracks into which you can place video and audio on a timeline.

3. Add titles, transitions, and effects. You create these using the tools in the editing software and then apply them to the video, audio, and still images that make up the video. The ease and flexibility of such tools distinguish the various brands of video editors.

4. Compress and save the video. With most editors, the video is compressed as it is saved. (A discussion of compression schemes and file formats is included later in this section.)

Preparing the Elements: Video

Figure 5.4 A Video-Editing Program

High-end systems for video editing include those from Avid Corporation and from Media 100. These expensive hardware and software combinations are used for professional-quality video post-production and are designed to produce broadcast-quality video for television. Most video for Web sites is edited with midrange software such as Final Cut Pro from Apple or Premiere from Adobe Corporation. These programs work on standard desktop personal computers. The fastest-growing video editor is Apple's iMovie. This software is shipped on Macintosh computers with DV (FireWire) input and can produce video suitable for Web sites. EditDV from Digital Origin provides similar capabilities on Windows computers.

Video Size

Unlike television, video on the Web usually cannot play full-screen and full-motion. For most users, the video will appear in a window whose size depends on users' bandwidth and the speed of their computer's processor and video system. The day is coming when Web video will look just like television, but today it's possible only with the latest computer on a very fast network.

Table 5.2 reflects the current state of Web video technology, which allows medium-quality video at the sizes and frame rates shown for users with the specified bandwidths.

Table 5.2 Web Video Technology

Connection	Bandwidth	Size (Pixels)	Frame Rate
56K modem	50 kbs	160×120	8
DSL or cable modem	500 kbs	320×240	12
Ethernet	10 MB	640×480	15

As you save your video file, you must take into account the nature of the target users' connections. Save the file at a size and frame rate that can be received by a typical viewer.

Frame Rate

On television, video plays at 30 frames per second. At this rate, even fast motion and quick pans appear smooth. But video digitized at 30 frames per second (fps) creates very large files that take a long time to download, so most video on the Web is run at 12 or 15 fps. The jumpy or jerky motion of this lower frame rate is noticeable only during quick motion, pans, and zooms. As bandwidth and video system speeds increase, the frame rate of Web video will improve.

You must match the frame rate of your video to the technical capabilities of the target audience. If your users have high-speed connections and new, powerful computers and need high-quality video, you may need to specify a rate of 30 fps. But for most users, even those with cable and DSL connections, you won't be able to transmit more than 15 fps. In fact, if you try to send 30-fps video to a user with a slow connection, the quality of the video will be much worse than if you send 10- or 12-fps video.

Video Compression

Video compression for the Web deserves a book of its own. As you saw earlier, there are a variety of codecs for video—even more than for sound—from a variety of vendors, all competing to deliver the highest-quality picture at the lowest data rate.

Needless to say, video must be compressed to flow through the Web. A single frame of video, at a typical size for the Web of 320 by 240 pixels, contains 76,800 pixels. If each pixel's color is represented by a 16-bit number, that's 1,228,800 bits of data per frame. At 15 frames per second, a minute of video would send 1,105,920,000 bits of data across the Internet. That's too much. A 56K modem would take more than five hours to download such a file!

The same video, compressed with, say, the Sorenson Video codec, can be reduced by a factor of 100. As a result, it might download in less than a minute.

Video compression is not magic; it's math. Most of the pixels in a typical video stream do not change from frame to frame. Picture the seven o'clock news. Dan Rather sits at his desk and reads the story. His lips move, and sometimes his eyebrows. But the CBS logo, the desk, and the background are static—identical from one moment to the next. Looking at such a file from the computer's point of view, you'd see the same pattern of numbers (pixels) repeating from frame to frame. Only a few numbers change each time. The video compressor software looks at this pattern of numbers and remembers only those that change. For the rest, it simply records "ditto."

You don't need to manipulate or understand the arcane details of video compression algorithms. But you do need to match the compression scheme to the needs and situations of your audience. To ensure that the greatest number of your site visitors can receive your video, you should use one of the three mainstream video systems—RealVideo, QuickTime, or Windows Media—with one of its built-in codecs. Remember that the more a file is compressed, the lower its quality. To make the video work well on the computers of the target audience, you may need to use a smaller size and lower frame rate as well as moderate compression.

For a listing of the video codecs currently available, visit the Terran Company's Web site at `http://terran-int.com/CodecCentral/Codecs/index.html`.

Table 5.3 lists some of the widely used video file formats, codecs, and how they are used.

Table 5.3 Widely Used Video File Formats

File Format	File Extension	Codecs	Application
RealVideo	`.ram`	RealVideo	Any application, wide range of quality settings
QuickTime Movie	`.mov`	Sorenson, Cinepak, Motion JPEG, H.263, DV, many others	Any application, wider range of quality settings
Windows Media	`.asf`	Windows Media	Any application, wide range of quality settings

Saving Video Files

You should save video files in the format, and with the file extension, appropriate to the system you're using to serve the video. For each system, you use a slightly different method:

☆ To create a RealVideo file, save the clips from your video-editing in QuickTime or AVI format. Then open them in RealProducer and save them in the RealVideo format with the `.ram` extension. You must save the files in a special directory on the RealVideo server. They cannot reside on your regular Web server.

☆ You can save QuickTime video files directly from video-editing software such as Adobe Premiere, iMovie, Final Cut Pro, or Media Cleaner Pro. You save regular video in the video folder on your Web server. You must save streaming video files with a streaming track and place them in the appropriate directory on the QuickTime streaming server. All QuickTime files are saved with the `.mov` extension.

☆ You must open Windows Media files with the Windows Media Encoder program and then save them with the `.asf` extension in the appropriate directory on the Windows Media Services NT server.

☆ **TIP**   As you save these files, keep careful track of their filenames and locations. You will need this information when you assemble the Web pages that contain the video.

☆ **DO IT YOURSELF**   **Prepare Video Files**

Prepare any video files necessary to your Web site, following the approaches described above.

◎◎ Preparing the Elements: Forms and Databases

One way to collect feedback from your site visitors is to provide a form where they enter and submit information. A simple data collection system might let users send a few items to the Web master in an e-mail. In a more complex system, you might save the items from the form into a database, where they can be compiled and acted on. Either way, you must prepare the form elements and the database before you assemble the Web page.

For simple e-mail data collection, your preparation consists mainly of designing the form itself. You need a list of the desired items, the form type for each one, and the e-mail address where the data will be sent.

If the data will be sent to a database, you must build the database and then build the form elements from the database.

Designing a Database

Using a database program such as FileMaker, Access, MySQL, or Oracle, you set up **fields** to contain each item of data to be collected. Figure 5.5 shows a form for collecting a user's name and other basic information.

The fields in the database for this form are Last Name, First Name, Film Title, Director, and so forth. Each time a user submits this form from the Web page, a new record is added to the database. After it's built, the database is run on a server that is connected to the Internet and linked to a URL.

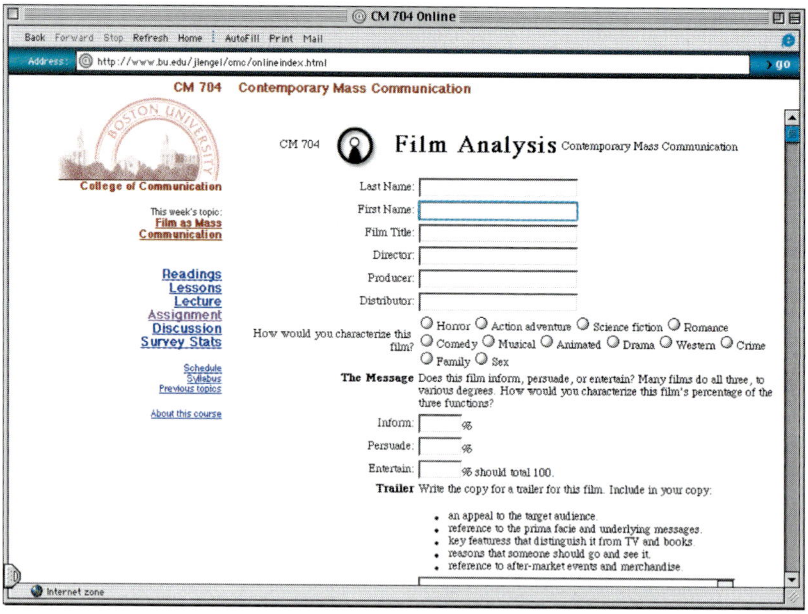

Figure 5.5 Form for Collecting Information

Building a Form

Most Web designers use a specially designed software program to build the Web page form from the database and to generate the code that links the form items to the database. The program bridges the gap between the Web page and the database. Examples of such programs are ColdFusion, FileMaker Web Companion, and Interdev. The program reads the necessary information from the database and then allows you to choose how to display each field as a form element on a Web page. It outputs a file of HTML code that adds the user-entered data to the correct fields in the database. The code might look like this:

```
<FORM ACTION="FMPro" METHOD="post">
<P><INPUT TYPE="hidden" NAME="-DB" VALUE="filmanalysis">
<INPUT TYPE="hidden" NAME="-Lay" VALUE="Layout #1">
<INPUT TYPE="hidden" NAME="-format"
VALUE="new_reply.htm">
<INPUT TYPE="hidden" NAME="-error"
VALUE="new_error.htm"></P>
<CENTER><TABLE BORDER=0>
    <TR>
<TD ALIGN=center><P>CM 704</P></TD>
<TD ALIGN=center WIDTH=68><P><IMG SRC="images/fmab.gif"
WIDTH=41 HEIGHT=41 ALIGN=middle></P></TD>
<TD ALIGN=center><P><FONT SIZE="+3"><B>Film
```

```
Analysis</B></FONT></P></TD>
<TD ALIGN=center><P>Contemporary Mass
Communication</P></TD>
  </TR>
</TABLE>
<TABLE BORDER=0 WIDTH="100%">
  <TR>
<TD WIDTH="33%"><P></P></TD>
<TD><P></P></TD>
  </TR>
  <TR>
<TD WIDTH="33%"><P ALIGN=right>Last Name:</P></TD>
<TD><P><INPUT TYPE=text NAME="Last Name" VALUE=""
SIZE=30></P></TD>
  </TR>
  <TR>
<TD WIDTH="33%"><P ALIGN=right>First Name:</P></TD>
<TD><P><INPUT TYPE=text NAME="First Name" VALUE=""
SIZE=30></P></TD>
  </TR>
```

When placed in a Web page, this HTML code displays the form and handles the submission of data to the database.

Standard Form Elements

The elements of a form serve various purposes. As shown in Figure 5.6, a **field** is used to hold short pieces of information entered from the keyboard, such as a name or an address. A **text area** (the Comments area in the figure) allows for longer entries and accommodates more than one line. A **radio button** lets the user select from a mutually exclusive set of choices, such as gender or age range. **Check boxes** let users click more than one choice in a series. An **option menu** lets the user use the mouse to choose from a list of items that appears when the menu is pressed. A **submit button** lets the user click to send the entire contents of the form to the database. A **reset button** clears the form of all its entries so that the user can start from scratch.

After you've designed the form, built the database, and generated the form code, you should test the operation of the form. Open the HTML code with a browser, fill in the form, click the submit button, and send the information to the database. Then look into the database to see whether the data arrived safely and in the proper place.

When the form is working properly, save the HTML file carefully because you'll need it when you assemble the Web page in the next step. The database should be left running on the server.

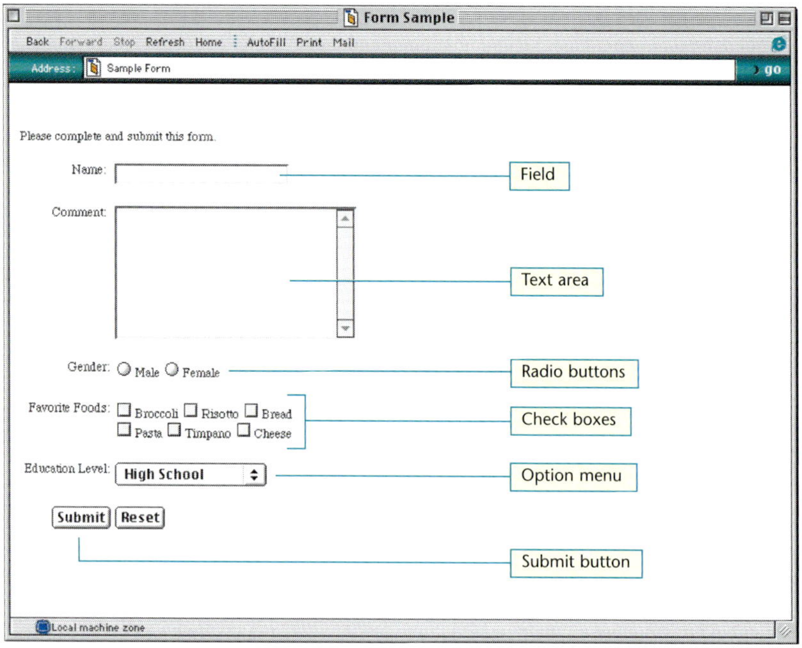

Figure 5.6 Form Elements

☆ **DO IT YOURSELF**   **Prepare Forms**

Prepare any forms needed for your Web site and, if required, prepare databases to receive the data generated by the forms.

Next Steps

At this point, you've prepared, sifted, and stirred the ingredients, and they're sitting on the counter waiting to be assembled into a meal. The hardest part of your job is finished. The next step, explained in Chapter Six, is to combine the ingredients into a tasty and attractive dish.

⭐ Summary

▷ To prepare animations, you use a variety of software tools to serve the particular functions of your Web site.

▷ To be successfully employed in a Web site, sound must be carefully recorded, edited, compressed, and saved in a format suitable for the target audience.

▷ Video calls for high-bandwidth connections and special plug-ins, but it can be prepared and compressed to make it available to higher numbers of Web users.

▷ Response forms on a Web page send information to either an e-mail address or a database. The latter arrangement requires advance preparation of both the database and the form design.

⭐ Online References

To learn more about sound and video technologies, consult the sites of the three top purveyors of multimedia plug-ins and file formats:

Apple QuickTime: http://www.apple.com/quicktime/

RealNetworks: http://www.realnetworks.com/

Windows Media: http://www.microsoft.com/windows/windowsmedia/

⭐ Review Questions

1. How many content elements exist on a typical corporate Web page?

2. What programs are used to prepare animations for a Web page?

3. Why do sound and video files need to be compressed for use on a Web page?

4. Explain the trade-off between bandwidth and video quality on the Web.

☆ Hands-On Exercises

1. Connect to a corporate Web page. Download each of the separate elements onto your computer. Explain the purpose, file format, and method of preparation for each element.

2. Download a simple animation from the Web, and analyze it to determine the number of frames or elements it contains.

3. Create a simple animation with GifBuilder, Flash, Fireworks, Photoshop, or Director.

4. Prepare a short sound or video file to be used on a Web page.

5. Design the fields for a simple database to collect information from the users of a Web site, and sketch what the form would look like on the screen.

CHAPTER SIX

SELECTING TOOLS, ORGANIZING FILES, AND CREATING TEMPLATES

This chapter introduces the various types of Web-page creation tools and explains how to organize the files that make up your site. It also points out the differences between the various methods of building a site and the kinds of software that are used for each approach, offering guidance to help you choose the most appropriate tools. The chapter describes the functions of Hypertext Markup Language and explains how the Web-page building tools create HTML code. It also describes how to create templates, which help you save time by automatically producing the repeated display elements in your site.

Chapter Objectives

⭐ To understand the kinds of software tools that are used to build a Web site

⭐ To understand the role of the Web designer in creating a site

⭐ To learn how to organize the elements of your site so that they can be assembled properly

★ To use templates, tables, and frames as appropriate to lay out your site

Basic Tool Types for Building Your Site

A cook employs a variety of tools to create the meal. She uses a bowl to mix, a skillet to sauté, an oven to bake, and a pot to boil. Not every meal calls for every implement; sometimes all you need is to pop a package into the microwave. Similarly, you employ a variety of software tools to assemble a Web page. Some tools are easy to learn and use, whereas others require considerable study and practice. Selecting the right tools to execute the design of your Web site is an important consideration.

There must be fifty ways to make a Web page. Mel might use HTML. Dave might try a little Shockwave. Mr. Cleaver might use Dreamweaver, and Clive might do it with GoLive. Rip might write some JavaScript, while Phil makes it with PageMill. While Ferd might export from Word, a sage would try FrontPage. Just pick a tool and go.

It's not quite that easy. The best tool for you is the one that fits your skill level and at the same time allows you to build the functions called for in your design. Web page assembly tools fall into three types:

★ **WYSIWYG editors:** These provide a blank page into which you import the elements that you have prepared, and they give you tools for formatting the page and making links between pages. PageMill, GoLive, FrontPage, and Dreamweaver are examples of WYSIWYG ("what you see is what you get") editors.

★ **Code editors:** These assist you in authoring the HTML, XML, or Javascript code that forms the Web page. They are like specialized word processors. You can't see the page itself, only the code that you are writing. HomeSite, BBEdit, and HotDog Pro are examples of code editors.

★ **Save As HTML functions of other programs:** To create very simple Web pages, you can click Save As HTML under the File menu of programs such as Microsoft Word. This command creates a Web page from the content of the word-processing document.

Anyone who can use a word processor can create a Web page using the Save As HTML function of Microsoft Word. But to use a code editor, you need to know the vocabulary and syntax of the code, understand how to write it, and understand how the code translates into the Web page elements. This is not for everyone. Between these two extremes lies the WYSIWYG editor, which can be learned quickly and requires no coding or programming knowledge.

If you assemble your pages with Microsoft Word, your design choices are limited. You can create only what you see in the word processor. Your design choices are almost unlimited if you use a code editor because the code is flexible and extensible. With a WYSIWYG editor, you can build almost everything mentioned and illustrated in this book but perhaps not exactly in the way you want.

The working environments for the three types of Web authoring tools are quite different. You're probably familiar with the working environment of a word processor.

Unless you're a computer programmer, though, a Web page code editor environment (see Figure 6.1) will probably seem incomprehensible. Not all code editors look like the one shown in the figure. Many HTML authors write their code in a simple text editor such as WordPad or SimpleText, which show only the code and include no extra windows or tools.

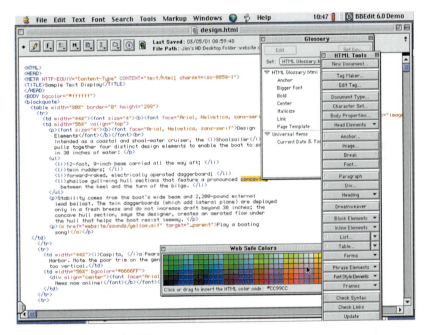

Figure 6.1 BBEdit Code Editor

A WYSIWYG editor (see Figure 6.2) looks like a word processor with extra windows, parameters, and menu items.

Although these tools seem quite different, all of them perform the same function: They create a file that contains the text of the Web page as well as instructions on how to construct and display the page. This file of instructions is opened and interpreted by a Web browser, such as Netscape or Explorer. The file does not contain the images, animations, sounds, or videos themselves; it only tells the browser where to go to get the elements and how to display them on the page. That's why it's crucial to organize your files carefully, as explained later in this chapter.

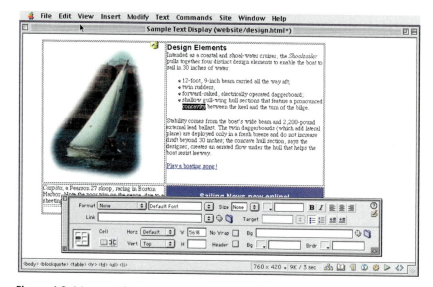

Figure 6.2 Macromedia Dreamweaver WYSIWYG Editor

These instructions are usually written in HTML code, although some Web pages may use JavaScript code. The Web assembly software must somehow generate this file of instructions. With a code editor this is straightforward: The code that you write is the actual set of instructions that ends up in the file. With the other two tools, the program converts the WYSIWYG page or the Word document into a set of coded instructions.

⭐ **DO IT YOURSELF**   **Select the Right Tool**

Which Web page building environment is best suited to the development of your site? Consider the nature of your site, the availability of software, and your own programming skills, and choose the tool that best fits your needs.

Behind the Scenes: HTML and Scripts

For most Web designers and certainly for the audience of your Web site, HTML and JavaScript code are behind-the-scenes actors. The user never sees it. In many cases, the author never sees it. It's like the back pantry in a fine restaurant, where the cabbage is sliced and the chickens are gutted: Few people observe what's going on, but everybody eats the products. And the restaurant could not survive without it.

Consider the typical Web page shown in Figure 6.3.

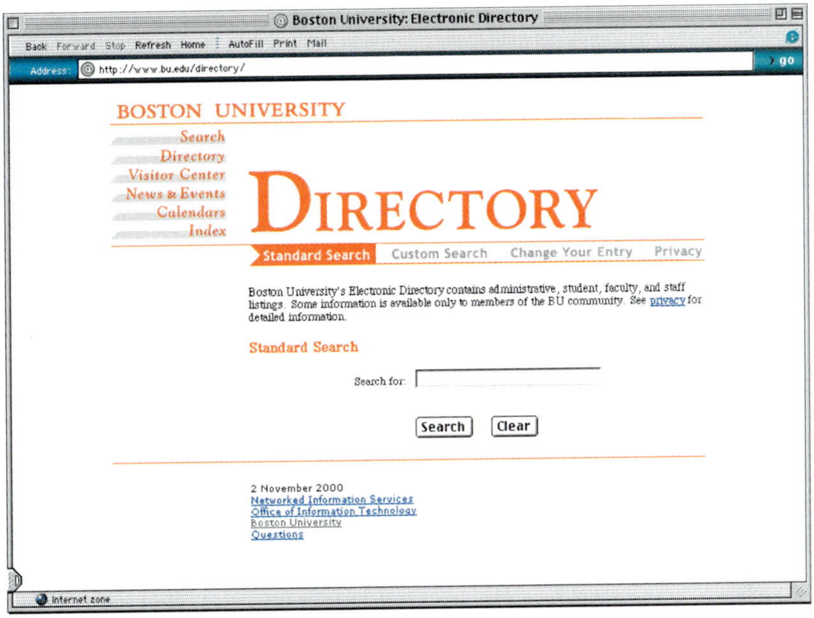

Figure 6.3 A Typical Web Page

Here is some of the HTML code that was used to create the page in Figure 6.3:

```
<html>
<head>
<title>Boston University: Electronic Directory</title>
...
</head>
<body bgcolor="#FFFFFF" text="#000000" link="#025BA4"
vlink="#666666" alink="#808000">
<table width="586" border="0" cellspacing="0"
cellpadding="0" align="center">
...
<tr><td><a href="/" onMouseOut="MM_swapImgRestore()"
onMouseOver="MM_swapImage('buhome','','graphics/
banner-topleftx.gif',1)"><img src="graphics/
banner-topleft.gif" width="240" height="27" alt="Boston
University home page" border="0" name="buhome"></a></td>
...
<p>Boston University's Electronic Directory contains
administrative, student, faculty, and staff listings.
Some information is available only to members of the
BU community. See <a href="privacy.html">privacy</a>
```

```
for detailed information. </p>
<h3><font color="#CC0000">Standard Search</font></h3>
<form action="http://www.bu.edu/htbin/webph/query.pl"
method="POST">
<center><input type="hidden" name="area"
value="directory" CHECKED>Search for: 
<input type="text" name="search_for" value="" size=35>
</center>
<p> <center>
<input type="Submit" value=" Search " name="Submit">
<input type="Reset" value=" Clear " name="Reset">
</center>
</form>
```

Table 6.1 analyzes what this code accomplishes. Remember that each word in the code is an instruction to the browser about how to set up the Web page. Here, the Javascript code is shown on a blue background to differentiate it from the HTML.

Table 6.1 Selected Code for the Site in Figure 6.3

Code	What It Does
```html <head> <title>Boston University: Electronic Directory</title> … </head>```	Puts the words "Boston University: Electronic Directory" into the title bar of the browser window.
```<body bgcolor="#FFFFFF" text="#000000" link="#025BA4" vlink="#666666" alink="#808000"```	Sets the background color to white, sets the color of the text to black, and sets the colors of link text to blue, gray, and purple.
```<table width="586" border="0" cellspacing="0" cellpadding="0" align="center">```	Sets up a table 586 pixels wide, with invisible borders, and places it in the center of the page.
```<tr><td><a href="/" onMouseOut="MM_swapImgRestore()" onMouseOver="MM_swapImage('buhome', '','graphics/banner-topleftx.gif', 1)"><img src="graphics/ banner-topleft.gif" width="240" height="27" alt="Boston University home page" border="0" name="buhome"></a></td>```	Adds a row to the table and, in the first column of that row, sets up a hypertext link back to the home page. Then it places a 240 by 27-pixel image (banner-topleft.gif) into the table. (This image is a picture of the words "BOSTONUNIVERSITY" that you see at the top of the page.) It also sets up a second image to be displayed when the user rolls the mouse over the first one (called a **rollover**); and it

	provides some text to be displayed in case the viewer's browser can't load the images.
`<p>`Boston University's Electronic Directory contains administrative, student, faculty, and staff listings. Some information is available only to members of the BU community. See `<a href= "privacy.html">`privacy`</a>` for detailed information. `</p>`	Displays a paragraph of text on the page and sets up a hypertext link from the word *privacy* to another Web page called `privacy.html`.
`<h3><font color="#CC0000">` Standard Search`</font></h3>` `<form action= "http://www.bu.edu/ htbin/webph/query.pl" method="POST"><center>`	Displays the words *Standard Search* in big red letters and then sets up a form to collect information from users. The form contents will be sent (posted) to the database on the "webph" server.
`<input type="hidden" name="area" value="directory" CHECKED>`Search for: `<input type="text" name= "search_for" value="" size=35> </center><p><center> <input type="Submit" value=" Search " name="Submit">` `<input type="Reset" value=" Clear " name="Reset"> </center> </form>`	Sends a hidden instruction to the database server to search the directory, displays the words *Search for:*, sets up an empty 35-character-wide text input field, and then adds Submit and Reset buttons, all centered on the page.

By studying Figure 6.3 and Table 6.1, you can see how the instructions produce the page. This set of instructions might have been produced by a programmer writing the code from scratch in a code editor, or it might have been produced by using a WYSIWYG editor. But it could not have been built in Word and then saved as HTML because Word cannot create JavaScript rollovers or data input forms.

It doesn't matter whether the Web designer uses a code editor or a WYSIWYG editor. The end result is a file of instructions in HTML that lets the audience's browser display the desired elements on the page.

On Center Stage: Page-Editing Environments and Tools

Other books in the Web Wizard series provide instruction in writing HTML, JavaScript, XML, and other kinds of code that can be used to assemble Web pages. Because this book concentrates on design, its examples use a WYSIWYG editor. The various editors look different and work differently, but all of them share a large set of common features and methods of assembly. The marketplace for WYSIWYG page-editing software is competitive and volatile, with new entries arriving regularly and updates vying to offer the latest features. But almost all of these products include the following:

★ A document window: This is the blank window into which you import, display, and arrange the page elements. What you see in the document window looks similar to, but not exactly the same as, what the user will see in the browser window.

★ Layout tools: You use these tools to create the frames, tables, and backgrounds that form the structure of the Web page. You **invoke** (activate) these tools by using menu commands, toolbars, palettes, or floating windows.

★ Text tools: You use these tools to type, paste, or import text, place it on the page, and then modify its size, weight, color, font, style, and alignment, much as in a word processor.

★ Import facilities: With these tools, you can import images, tabular data, sound, video, Java applets, animations, and other elements and embed them into the page.

★ Image tools: After you import an image, you use these tools to resize and align the image and to create **images** that have **hot spots** that link to another page.

★ Multimedia tools: You use these tools to control the way sound or video is displayed: How big will the video image be? Will the page include a controller? Will the sound or video play automatically or wait for the user to click it? Will it play once or loop forever?

★ Linking tools: You use these tools to create a link from a word or element to another place on this page, to another page on the site, or to another URL on the Web. You can also specify where and how the linked page will be displayed.

★ Site management tools: When the page is complete, you use these tools to save it to the proper place on the server or local disk and to keep track of the locations of all the elements. Some programs even support page templates (discussed later in this chapter) and multiple-page editing.

Figure 6.4 shows a page editor with some of these tools invoked and ready for use.

Each editor names and organizes these tools in a slightly different way and provides its own methods of adjusting and controlling the page elements. For most Web pages, you won't need to use all or even most of these tools. Later in this chapter, you'll follow the steps in building a simple Web page and learn how each tool accomplishes its task.

A good Web-authoring software environment is like a kitchen outfitted with the best cookware and utensils. Some are hiding in drawers, others are hanging on the wall, and still others are stored in the shelves. It's the job of the *chef de cuisine* to figure out which tool to use, and in what order, to create a masterpiece.

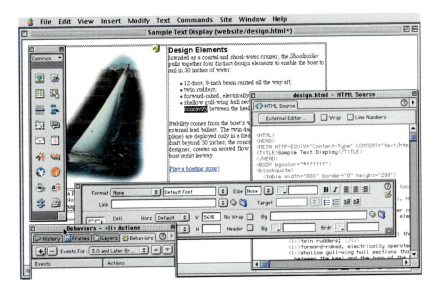

Figure 6.4 Editing Tools in Dreamweaver

◎◎ Directing the Action: The Role of the Web Designer

The Web designer is the chief cook and bottle-washer in the development and assembly of the Web site. It's the designer's task to see that the planned design and functions of the site are carried out and that the site as published accomplishes its purposes. No matter who actually does the work or which tools are used, the designer takes responsibility for the execution.

The first step is to begin with a clear specification of what is to be built—a blueprint to be used to guide the process of building the pages. The specification should include the following:

⭐ A list of the purposes of the site and of the page or section being built (see Chapters One, Two, and Three)

⭐ A description of the target audience, including their technical capabilities and typical system setup

⭐ A sketch of the Web page, with callouts explaining the various elements

⭐ A list of functions for the page

⭐ A list of the elements and their filenames

⭐ A description of the organization of directories (folders) that contain the site's files

These specifications should be supplied and explained to the person who builds the pages for the site.

The next section describes how to turn these specs into a Web site. It is wise to keep track of the building process periodically. Just as the master chef tastes the concoctions prepared by the sous chefs, so must the Web designer check to see that the design is being executed faithfully.

☆ **TIP**   **Milestones**

To help manage the site-building process, establish milestones that call for a daily or weekly inspection of the site as it is being built.

A standard practice is to build one entire section of the site first. Then you use this section to test functionality and user reaction. Problems or issues that arise can be addressed at this point, and the design can be modified as necessary, before all the pages have been built. Chapter Eight explains how to test and review your site.

The remainder of this chapter describes how to organize the elements, and Chapter Seven describes how to assemble and link the pages.

◎◎ Organizing the Elements

Just before starting to cook, the chef arranges the ingredients carefully on the counter, each one in its labeled container and ready to deploy into the cooking vessels. The Web designer must do the same thing, organizing the elements into their folders and giving them their proper filenames. The chef, however, seldom has to manufacture his own pots and pans, but the Web designer must sometimes create templates for the Web pages.

It's time to take out the flow chart you created in Chapter One, examine the folders that contain the elements, and organize them so that you (and, more important, the Web server) know where everything is located. The images, with their file extensions of `.gif`, `.jpg`, or `.png`, should be in the images folder. The videos and sounds, with proper file extensions, should be in their respective folders. You should also have a list of the filenames that you plan to use for the Web pages themselves. Figure 6.5 shows a typical situation at this point.

The Web pages that you are about to build (the `.htm` or `.html` files) are saved in the Web site folder, as shown in Figure 6.5. For now, these files and folders are saved on your own computer. Later, when your site is complete, they will be posted to the Web server using the same directory structure.

☆**WARNING** After you start building the site, it's difficult to change the names of any of the files or folders because the links are based on the files' **pathnames**. The pathname of a file consists of the name of the computer it's on, the name of the directory (folder) and subdirectories it's in, and finally the filename. The pathname for one of the image files in the example shown in Figure 6.5, for example, might be `webserver/website/images/boathouse.jpg`. At this point, make sure all your files and folders are named correctly and that all of the files are in the right place.

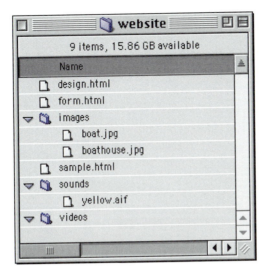

Figure 6.5 Typical Web Site Directory Structure

Web Servers

A Web server is a computer connected to the Internet that sends files to other computers that request them. Theoretically, any computer can be a Web server as long as it's connected to the Internet and is running Web server software. Realistically, most organizations set up a computer dedicated to serving Web sites. It runs 24 hours a day and has a robust Internet connection.

Few Web designers use the Web server to build their sites. Instead, they build the site on their own computer, test it, and then copy it to the Web server when it's complete.

Web servers are usually managed by an organization's information technology (IT) department. Typically, only authorized users can access the Web server and post Web sites.

☆**SHORTCUT**   Some Web-editing programs let you run two copies of your site as you build it: one on your own computer and a second one on the Web server. This arrangement lets you test both of them during assembly.

☆**DO IT YOURSELF**   **Organize the Files**

Organize the files for your Web site, ensuring that filenames are in the proper form and that you know exactly what each file contains.

Using Templates, Tables, and Frames

In your site sketch you may have worked up a common framework that will appear on all the pages. This might include a common menu bar, a consistent columnar structure, a background graphic, or a header or footer that you want to appear on every page. If such a framework is important to your design, it's a good idea to build it before you assemble the pages. You can combine these elements into a **template**, a file that contains all the common elements but none of the page-specific content. Figure 6.6 shows a template for a simple Web site.

Figure 6.6 Template for a Web Site

This template includes the site name in big letters across the top, a menu bar down the left side, three logos, and a white rectangle for the content. All the pages in this site share this template.

You can build a template using a table or a frameset. A **table** is a grid that divides the space on the page into rows and columns. A **frameset** creates a page with several frames, each of which displays a different file.

Template with Tables

The template in Figure 6.6 was built using tables. The main table contains two columns and two rows. The left column contains logos and the menu items, and the right column contains the corporate name and the content text. Three of the cells in this table are set to a dark red background, and the fourth is left white. The lower-right cell contains a second table whose width (450 pixels) constrains the text to a readable line width. You can build such a table directly in HTML or use a WYSIWYG editor. Figure 6.7 shows how the table was configured.

| This cell is merged with the cell below, so it has a row span of 2. It contains two logos, seven menu items, and another logo at the bottom. Its background color is set to dark red #990000, and its width is set to 150 pixels. The text for the menu items is set in Verdana bold size 1 white. | This cell contains the corporate title. It is set to a fixed height of 40 pixels. The title is set in Verdana bold size 5 white. The background color is set to dark red #990000. |
| | This cell has no background color. It contains another table with a fixed width of 450 pixels to display the content text. The title is set in Verdana bold size 3 black, and the body text is set in Georgia size 3 black. |

Figure 6.7 Tables Used to Build the Template in Figure 6.6

The Web page itself is set with no margins. The table is set with no cell padding, no cell spacing, no borders, and a width and height of 100%, so it aligns with the edge of the browser window and displays no lines between its cells. To build such a table in a WYSIWYG editor, follow these steps:

1. Open a new page.
2. Set the page properties to make all margins equal to zero.
3. Insert a table.
4. Set the properties of the table as follows:
   - Width = 100%, height = 100% (the table will fill the browser window, no matter how big the window is)
   - Border = 0 (no borders will show inside or outside the table)
   - Cellspacing = 0, cellpadding = 0 (items placed in the cells will align with the edge)

The HTML code for this table looks like this:

```
<body leftmargin="0" topmargin="0" marginwidth="0"
marginheight="0">
<table width="100%" border="0" cellspacing="0"
cellpadding="0" height="100%">
```

After the table is built, each cell is set with the proper background color, height, width, and row span. Then you place the text and images into each cell and set them to the appropriate font style, size, and color. Along the way, you check the design often by previewing it in the browser window.

When complete, this template page is saved as an HTML file that is used to build all the other pages in the site. In this way, the pages share a common format and menu set. Only the text in the lower-right cell of the table changes as the user moves from page to page.

★ **SHORTCUT**   Many WYSIWYG editors include a Save As Template feature that makes it easy to create a template and lets you update the template even after the pages have been built.

Template with Frames

You can build a similar template as a frameset. The frameset page contains three frames. Two of them (the title and the menu) remain the same as the third one (the content) changes. The same template, executed as a frameset, would look like Figure 6.8.

Many Web editors provide tools for building framesets like this. Using Dreamweaver, a typical WYSIWYG page editor, you would follow these steps (see Figure 6.9):

1. Click New from the File menu to create a new document window.

2. Click Frames from the Insert menu to set up a frame on the left, right, top, or bottom.

3. Insert other frames as appropriate.

4. In the Frames window, type a name for each frame.

5. Into each frame insert the graphics, text, background colors, and other elements that will be common to all pages. (The content of each frame will be saved as a separate HTML file.)

6. Preview the frameset in your Web browser, and adjust it if necessary.

7. Save the frameset as an HTML file.

8. Save each frame page as an HTML file. (In Dreamweaver, when you save the frameset, the program prompts you to save each of the component HTML files.)

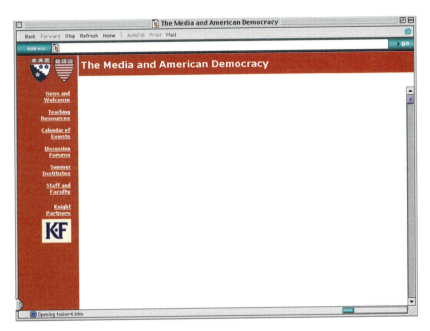

Figure 6.8 Template Built as a Frameset

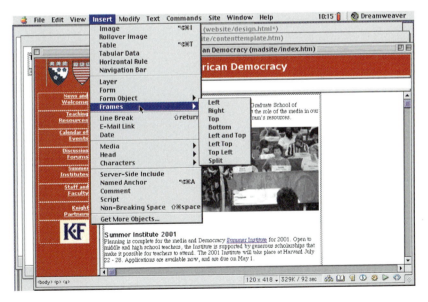

Figure 6.9 Building a Frameset with Dreamweaver

☆**WARNING** Using a frameset to build a template is more complicated than using a table. For users, a site displayed in multiple frames can sometimes cause navigational problems and can make it hard to bookmark individual pages. A site built around a table-based template does not create these kinds of potential problems for designers or users.

☆**TIP**   **Using Specialized Templates**

If you're building a simple site, a single template will probably suffice. For a more complex site, you might want to use several templates—for example, one template for text pages, another one for pages that are mostly pictures, and another one for pages containing feedback forms.

☆**DO IT YOURSELF**   **Create a Template**

Using tables or frames as appropriate, build a template for the pages in your site. Save your template so that it can be used over and over again to create the various pages in your site.

⭐ Summary

▷ Web pages can be authored by using code editors or WYSI-WYG editors, or by saving Word documents as HTML. The choice of page-building tools depends on the nature of the site and the skills of the builder.

▷ No matter who builds the site, the Web designer is responsible for seeing to it that the site is constructed according to the design specifications.

▷ Files containing the site's various content and display elements must be properly organized and named before page building can begin.

▷ Page templates, built using tables or frames, give a consistent form to the various pages in a site.

⭐ Online References

ZDNet Developer. A site full of articles, ideas, and tools for the Web developer.
http://www.zdnet.com/devhead/filters/homepage/

CNET Builder.com. Excellent reviews and comparisons of various Web-authoring tools.
http://builder.cnet.com/webbuilding/0-3880.html?tag=sb

Dreamweaver information. Ideas and specifications on this WYSIWYG Web-authoring program from its publisher.
http://www.macromedia.com/software/dreamweaver/

Build a Web page with Microsoft Word. Tips and instructions from the publisher of this ubiquitous word-processing program.

Windows users visit
http://www.microsoft.com/office/word/websave.htm.

Macintosh users visit
http://www.microsoft.com/mac/products/office/2001/articles/articles_wd.asp?Language=EN&ID=109&Page=1&Ar=Word2001

⭐ Review Questions

1. Compare the three different types of authoring environments for building a Web page.

2. List at least five functions offered by most WYSIWYG editors.

3. Explain how the files for a site should be named and organized before building begins.

4. Describe the file extensions used for four media types.

5. When should a frame or table be used as a template for a Web page?

★ Hands-On Exercises

1. Use Microsoft Word to create a simple document, including a table and an image. Print a copy. Now go back and save it as a Web page. Open this file with a Web browser. Observe the differences between the two versions of the document.

2. Use a WYSIWYG editor to prepare a simple Web page with text, images, a table, and links.

3. Use a code or text editor to prepare the same page in Exercise 2 in HTML.

4. Gather the image, sound, and HTML files for your Web site, name them properly, and organize them into directories as shown in Figure 6.5.

5. Use the authoring tool of your choice to prepare a page built on a table-based template. Open the page with a browser.

6. Use the authoring tool of your choice to prepare a frameset and two Web pages. Open the frameset with a browser.

ASSEMBLING THE PAGES

This chapter explains how to assemble the various elements of a Web page and link the pages to create your Web site. If the aggregation of text, images, sounds, videos, and forms represents the ingredients of your site, consider this chapter the cooking lesson. You'll assemble, combine, and arrange the pieces into a complete meal ready to be presented to diners.

Chapter Objectives

- To learn how to create a page background using color, texture, or an image
- To discover how to lay out your pages using grids and borders
- To learn how to place text for maximum readability
- To learn how to display images in your site
- To learn how to embed and link sound and video
- To find out how to implement user-feedback forms
- To understand how to link Web pages to create a comprehensive Web site

◎◎ Creating Your Site's Background

The first step in building a Web page is to create the **background**. If the page design calls for a background image, such as a solid color or a washed-out picture that looks like a watermark, you set up the background first. On top of this background, you place any **tables** that you're using to divide the page into columns or grids to hold text and other elements. After that, you assemble the **content**: the text, images, sounds, videos, and forms that readers will interact with.

Typically, Web pages feature three kinds of backgrounds:

★ A solid color that sits behind the entire page

★ A textured color

★ A very light-colored, low-contrast image

Using Background Colors

If you're using a single solid color for your background, you program it as the page is built. It requires little or no extra memory or download time. But you must be careful to choose a color that is compatible with the colors of the company logo and other graphics. In addition, it must allow easy reading of the text.

★**WARNING** Midnight blue, blood red, and deep purple are great colors for establishing a mood, but you should think about how dark colors affect the readability of text. Reading more than a few words of light-colored text on a dark background is uncomfortable and inefficient. It can also cause problems in printing the page (white text won't be visible at all). Use deep, dark background colors only on pages that contain no text.

It's easy to set the background color of a Web page. In Dreamweaver and most other Web-page editors, you click Page Properties from the Modify menu. This opens a Page Properties dialog box. In this box, point the mouse to the word *background*, and choose a color from the palette. Click OK, and you will see the background in the document window.

The HTML code to set a background color would look like this:

```
<body bgcolor="#6666FF">
```

This code produces a blue background. The number #6666FF represents a shade of blue that's darker than the sky on a clear day at noon but lighter than the blue behind the stars in the American flag:

★**TIP**   **Seeing the Code**

Sometimes it's useful to see the HTML code that makes up a Web page. If you are viewing the page with a Web browser, click View Source under the View menu to open a new window in which the code is displayed. If you are working in a WYSIWYG editor such as Dreamweaver, open the HTML source window to see (and modify) the code that the editor is creating for you.

Using Background Images

A background image sits behind all the other elements, in a layer by itself. To use a background image, you prepare the image in Photoshop or another image-editing program and then import it into the Web page. It must be sized properly. To create a repeated texture such as that pictured in Figure 7.1, you begin with a small image, about 100 pixels square. You arrange it for a pleasant appearance and then **tile** it so that it's repeated in the background.

Figure 7.1 A Textured Background

The image displayed in the background of Figure 7.2 is sized to fill the entire page. The image is 800 pixels wide and 600 pixels high and fills the browser window of a standard computer display.

Both backgrounds were based on photographs and prepared in an image-editing program such as Photoshop. For the image in Figure 7.1, the designer adjusted its color settings and carefully selected one set of tracks so that it would tile well. The image in Figure 7.2 was given a washed-out appearance by adjusting contrast. The animal tracks were saved in GIF format, the boat in JPEG. When displayed on the Web page, both backgrounds communicate in a subtle way that quietly complements the contents of the page.

Be careful when you're selecting background images. In Figure 7.3, the background image is so distinct that it's almost impossible to read the text.

Figure 7.2 A Background Image

Figure 7.3 Confusing Background Image and Text

It's best to use an image or texture that's so washed out that it is barely recognizable. To wash out an image in Photoshop, use either the brightness and contrast controls or the hue and saturation settings. Click Adjust under the Image menu, and move the brightness up and the contrast down until the image looks right. Save background images in your images folder.

To set a background image with Dreamweaver, click Page Properties from the Modify menu. A Page Properties dialog box will open. Click the Choose button next to the background image field. This opens another dialog box where you can choose the image you want to use. Make sure you choose the image from the images folder in your Web site directory. Click OK to see the background image in the document window.

The HTML code to set a background image would look like this:

```
<body background= "images/bighouse.jpg">
```

In this example, the name of the image file is `bighouse.jpg`, and it is in the images folder.

☆ **DO IT YOURSELF**   **Create a Background**

Select or create a background for one of the pages in your site. Depending on your design, you might use a background color, a texture, or an image. Follow the instructions in this chapter to add the background to your page.

◎◎ Using Grids and Borders

If you want to display text or images in two or three columns or set aside a rectangle for a logo or menu bar, you can use a table. The table itself will be invisible, but it will provide a grid on which to place the various page elements. To hold text, for example, you might create a one-column, one-row table and fix its width to about 450 pixels. The result is a readable line of text, neither too wide nor too narrow. Or you might create a table containing one row and two columns, fixing the left column to 100 pixels (for a set of menu items) and the right to 450 pixels (for the page content).

In a WYSIWYG editor such as Dreamweaver, here's how to create such a table:

1. Click Table from the Insert menu.

2. In the Insert Table dialog box, set the number of rows and columns. Also, set the width of the table either in pixels or as a percentage of the user's window. Set the border to zero.

3. The table will be displayed in the document window. To change its appearance, you can click and drag the borders to stretch or shrink the table or its component cells.

4. Use the table's Properties window to set other table attributes, including the colors of the cells, the table's width and height, and the nature of its borders.

Here's the HTML code for a simple table:

```
<table width="550" border="0" height="400">
  <tr>
    <td width="100"></td>
    <td width="450"></td>
  </tr>
</table>
```

This code sets up a table 550 pixels wide and 400 pixels high, with invisible borders, and containing two columns, 100 and 450 pixels wide.

★ **SHORTCUT**   You don't necessarily need to create a table, especially for a simple Web page. Instead, you can place the elements directly on the page.

Now that the formatting is set up, you can place the content elements on the page.

★ **DO IT YOURSELF**   Format the Page

Create a simple table to format the text and other items on your Web page.

◎ Placing Readable Text

You can type text directly from the keyboard, copy it from another file and paste it into the Web page, or import it from HTML files created with Microsoft Word. You use the latter method when you want to preserve formatting from the original document.

No matter where it comes from, text must be displayed so that it's easy to read. In Chapter Two you learned some of the ways to design text so that it works well for readers. Now it's time to implement those suggestions.

The basic steps are as follows:

1. Type or paste the text into the right place. In a simple Web page, the text will appear directly on the page, starting in the upper-left corner and proceeding across the width of the window and down the page. If you have used a table to create a formatting grid, move the mouse pointer into the appropriate cell of the table and then type or paste the text.

2. Format the text for easy reading. Set a 12-point or larger serif font for the body text, and use a contrasting font for headings. Make headings and subheads heavier and larger than the body text. Leave white space around the column of text by indenting it. Adjust the width of the column to display 10 to 12 words per line. Format any bulleted or numbered lists that are called for in the site design.

3. Check the display of the text. What you see in the editor may not be what users will see, so preview the text by opening the page in Internet Explorer and then in Netscape. Also check it on both Macintosh and Windows platforms using the kinds of computers used by your target audience.

Your planning documents should tell you which text file to use, where it should be placed, and how it should be formatted. Locate and open these text files. Then open your Web page editor, and copy and paste the text into the page.

Here's how to place text using a WYSIWYG editor such as Dreamweaver:

1. Place the pointer at the spot in the Dreamweaver document window where you want the text to appear.

2. Type the text from the keyboard, or copy and paste it from the text file.

3. Format the text as called for in the design specification. Select the text, and then choose the appropriate item from the Text menu or from the Properties window.

4. To see how the text appears in Explorer and Netscape, click Preview in Browser from the File menu.

In HTML, plain text appears simply as text. But text with formatting picks up HTML tags that indicate its alignment, size, weight, and font style. Here is what an indented paragraph of text—with a subhead, a bulleted list, and an italicized word—would look like in HTML code:

```html
<blockquote>
  <p><font size="4"><b><font face="Arial, Helvetica,
sans-serif">Design Elements</font></b></font><br>
Intended as a coastal and shoal-water cruiser, the
<i>Shoalsailer</i> pulls together four distinct design
elements to enable the boat to sail in 30 inches of
water:</p>
<ul>
  <li>12-foot, 9-inch beam carried all the way aft;</li>
  <li>twin rudders; </li>
  <li>forward-raked, electrically operated daggerboard;
     </li>
  <li>shallow gull-wing hull sections that feature a
pronounced concavity between the keel and the turn of
the bilge. </li>
</ul>
  <p>Stability comes from the boat's wide beam and
2,200-pound external lead ballast. The twin daggerboards
(which add lateral plane) are deployed only in a fresh
breeze and do not increase draft beyond 30 inches; the
concave hull section, says the designer, creates an aer-
ated flow under the hull that helps the boat resist lee-
way. </p>
</blockquote>
```

Table 7.1 explains how each of the HTML tags modifies the text in this sample.

Table 7.1 HTML for Text in Figure 7.4

HTML Code	What It Does
`<blockquote>`	Indents the entire column of text to add some white space at the margin.
`<p><font size="4"><b>` `<font face="Arial, Helvetica,` `sans-serif"> Design Elements` `</font></b></font> `	Begins a new paragraph, sets the font size larger and boldface for this subtitle, sets a sans serif font, and adds a line break.

`Intended as a coastal and`
`shoal-water cruiser, the`
`<i>Shoalsailer</i> pulls`
`together four distinct design`
`elements to enable the boat to`
`sail in 30 inches of water:</p>`
	Displays a sentence of text with the word *Shoalsailer* in italics and then ends the paragraph.

`<ul>`
`  <li>12-foot, 9-inch beam`
`  carried all the way aft; </li>`
`  <li>twin rudders; </li>`
`  <li>forward-raked, electrically`
`  operated daggerboard; </li>`
`  <li>shallow gull-wing hull`
`  sections that feature a`
`  pronounced concavity between`
`  the keel and the turn of the`
`  bilge. </li>`
`</ul>`
	Displays a bulleted (unordered) list of four items.

`<p>Stability comes from the boat's`
`wide beam and 2,200-pound external`
`lead ballast. The twin daggerboards`
`(which add lateral plane) are`
`deployed only in a fresh breeze`
`and do not increase draft beyond`
`30 inches; the concave hull section,`
`says the designer, creates an`
`aerated flow under the hull that`
`helps the boat resist leeway. </p>`
	Displays a paragraph of plain text.

`</blockquote>`	Ends the indentation of the text.

◎◎ Displaying Useful Images

All your images should be saved in the site's images folder in the GIF, JPEG, or PNG format. Your site sketches should show you where to place the images. The task now is to get the images to appear in the proper place.

For a simple Web page containing one image and a paragraph of text, this is a straightforward task. You simply place the image before or after the text. An example is shown in Figure 7.4.

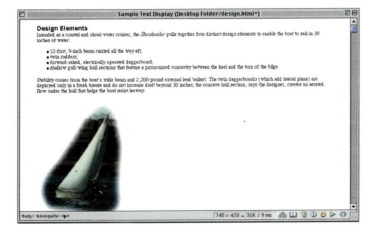

Figure 7.4 Simple Web Page with Text and Image

To create such a page using Dreamweaver, you would enter the text as described in the preceding section. Then place the pointer after the last paragraph, click Image from the Insert menu, find the desired picture, and watch it appear on the page.

Here's the HTML:

```
<img src="website/images/boat.jpg" width="200"
height="263">
```

This code tells the browser to place an image whose source is the file `boat.jpg` in the images folder, setting its size to 200 by 263 pixels. The image file's pathname is `website/images/boat.jpg`.

To place an image next to the text, rather than under it, you would move the image up so that it appears in front of the text, and then set the alignment of the image to the left. In Dreamweaver, you drag the image and then use the Properties window to set the alignment, as shown in Figure 7.5.

Figure 7.5 Image Properties Window Showing Alignment

In HTML, the picture would be tagged with left alignment:

```
<img src="website/images/boat.jpg" width="200"
height="263" align="left">
```

The resultant Web page would look like Figure 7.6.

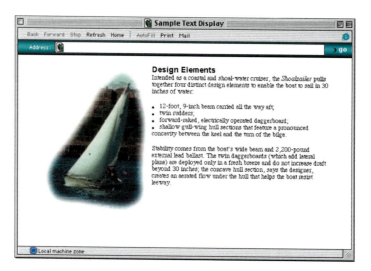

Figure 7.6 Web Page with Left-Aligned Image, and Text

This method of inserting and aligning images works well for simple Web pages. But for anything more complex, most Web designers use a table as a grid to guide the placement of images and text. To build the page just discussed, you create a table of two columns and one row and then insert the image into the left column and paste the text into the right column. For a Web page with multiple columns and images, using a table is a necessity. Figure 7.7 shows such a page being built in Dreamweaver. The grid lines that you see are for the designer only; users will not see them.

Figure 7.7 Using a Table in Dreamweaver to Place Text and Images

Using this technique, you can design a Web page that places the images and text as desired.

Embedding Sound and Video

Embedding a sound or video file into a page is very much like inserting an image. You insert the sound or video into the proper location on the page, and then you set its **parameters**. Parameters, also called **attributes**, include whether or not to display a controller, whether the sound or video will **loop** (repeat) or play only once, and whether it starts on its own or waits for the user to click.

In a Web editor such as Dreamweaver, follow these steps:

1. Place the pointer location on the page where the sound or video is to appear.

2. Click Media from the Insert menu, and then click Plug-in. (Sound and video files use browser plug-ins.)

3. Navigate to the sounds or video folder and find the desired sound or video file.

4. Insert the file. It will be represented as a plug-in icon. Size them appropriately.

5. To set the parameters of the sound or video, open its Properties window, click Parameters, and type the appropriate parameters.

6. Save the file, and then preview it in the browsers.

In the example shown in Figure 7.8, the designer has embedded a song with the filename `yellow.aif` into the page and has displayed a controller.

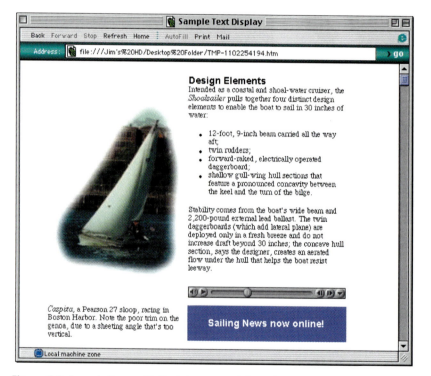

Figure 7.8 Sample Page with Text, Image, and Sound

Here's the HTML:

```
<embed src="website/sounds/yellow.aif" width="234"
height="29" controller="yes">
```

Notice the EMBED tag, the pathname to the sound file, and the width, height, and controller parameters. This sound was saved in the Audio Interchange File format with an `.aif` file extension.

You embed video in the same way, using the same steps in Dreamweaver and the same HTML code. By setting parameters for video and sound elements, you control how they appear and how users interact with them. Table 7.2 shows some of the commonly used parameters for sound and video.

Table 7.2 Sound and Video Parameters

Parameter	Values	Result
Autoplay	True or false	Makes the sound or video begin playing as soon as the page is viewed.
Controller	True or false	Shows a slider that lets the user stop, start, advance, or rewind the sound or video.
Height	Measurement in pixels	Sets the height of the display of the video; for sound, sets the height of the controller.
Hidden	True or false	Hides the file so that it does not display. Suitable only for sound files.
Loop	True or false	Plays the sound or movie repeatedly.
Width	Measurement in pixels	Sets the width of the display of the video; for sound, sets the width of the controller.

It is best to display video on a Web page at its original size, the size at which it was saved. Stretching or shrinking a video will distort its appearance and will severely affect its performance. For more information on displaying sound and video on a Web page, read *The Web Wizard's Guide to Multimedia*.

Linking to Sound and Video

Instead of embedding sound or video files in the page, the site design may call for them to open in their own window. To implement this, you create a link from a word or image on the Web page to the sound or video file, and you specify that it be opened in a new window.

In Dreamweaver or another WYSIWYG editor, you select the linking object and then click Make Link from the Modify menu. Select the sound or video file, and the link will be created. Use the Properties window to set the target for this link to New.

Here's the HTML code for this example of linked media:

```
<a href="website/sounds/yellow.aif" target="_new">Play a
boating song!</a>
```

This code sets up a hypertext reference to the `yellow.aif` sound file and opens a new window to play it in. In the next section you'll learn more about designing links.

☆ **DO IT YOURSELF**   **Embed Sound and Video**

If your Web site uses sound or video, embed or link it to the pages. Change the parameters to display these multimedia elements as called for in your design.

◎◎ Laying Out Forms

To place a user-feedback form in a Web page, you first set up a **form area**, and in that area you place form elements such as fields and buttons. You must also specify a **form action** that tells the browser where to send the data, and create a **submit button** for users to click to send the data they've entered.

In Dreamweaver, the process looks like this:

1. Click Form under the Insert menu to set up a form area on the page. It shows up as a dotted red rectangle.

2. Into this form area insert a form object by clicking Form Object from the Insert menu.

3. Use the Properties window to assign a name to the form object you just created.

4. Type instructions next to the form object, such as *Enter your name:*.

5. Insert more form objects as necessary. Make sure you place them within the red form area.

6. If you create radio buttons (where users make a mutually exclusive choice), all the buttons must have the same name but different values. For example, you might have two radio buttons named *Gender*, but one carries the value *Male*, and the other one *Female*. Use the Properties window to set the names and values of the form objects. The same process is used to create check boxes.

7. If you create an option list or menu, you can use the Properties window to enter the list items. You enter a label and a value for each item in the list.

8. Create a Submit button. Every form like this should have one.

9. To set the form action, first select the form (the red dotted line). In the Properties window, type `mailto:yourname@yourhost.net` into the Form action box. (Use the e-mail address where you want the feedback sent.) For data that's destined to be sent to a database, instead enter the URL and the name of the script or program that will process this information for the database.

10. Test your form by previewing it in both browsers.

Figure 7.9 shows a simple form created according to these steps.

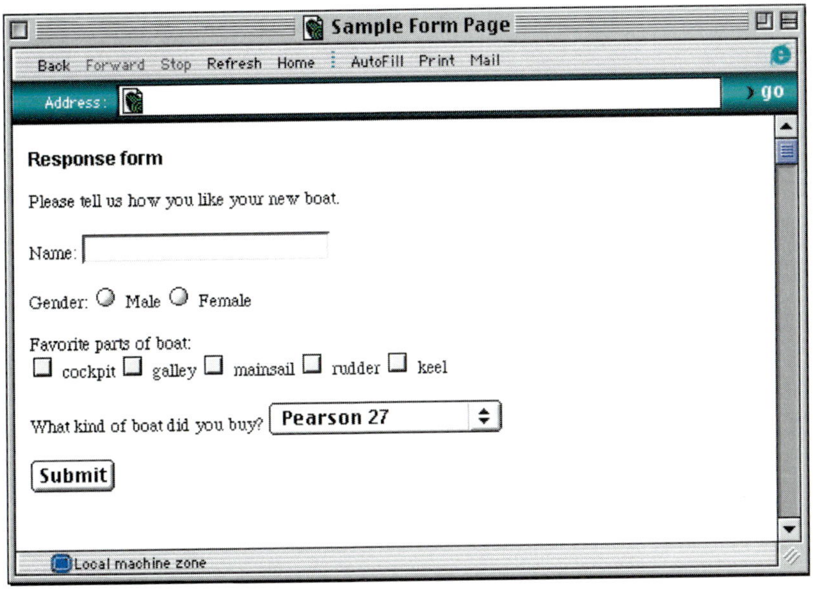

Figure 7.9 Sample Form

The HTML code for this page looks like this:

```
<html><head><title>Sample Form Page</title></head>
<body bgcolor="#FFFFFF">
<p><font face="Arial, Helvetica, sans-serif"><b>Response
form</b></font></p>
<p>Please tell us how you like your new boat.</p>
<form method="post" action="mailto:jlengel@bu.edu"
name="Boat response">
<p>Name: <input type="text" name="textfield"></p>
<p>Gender:
<input type="radio" name="gender" value="male">Male
<input type="radio" name="gender"
value="female">Female</p>
<p>Favorite parts of boat:<br>
<input type="checkbox" name="favorite"
value="cockpit">cockpit
<input type="checkbox" name="favorite"
value="galley">galley
<input type="checkbox" name="favorite"
value="mainsail">mainsail
```

```
<input type="checkbox" name="favorite"
value="rudder">rudder
<input type="checkbox" name="favorite"
value="keel">keel</p>
<p>What kind of boat did you buy?
    <select name="select">
      <option value="p27">Pearson 27</option>
      <option value="ae38">Alerion Express 38</option>
      <option value="c39">Concordia Yawl</option>
    </select></p>
  <p><input type="submit" name="Submit"
value="Submit"></p>
</form>
</body>
</html>
```

The new HTML tags (shown in blue backgound) involve forms: the **method** that the form will use, in this case posting data to a destination; the **action**, in this case mailing the data to the address specified; the various **input type**s (text, radio button, check box, and submit button); the **name**s and **value**s of each input; and the **select** item with its various **option**s.

☆**TIP**   Even a simple form like this can look better and be easier to use if it is formatted in a table, as you did with images in the preceding section. You use the table to separate the instructions from the form objects.

☆**DO IT YOURSELF**   **Add a Form**

Create a way for your audience to send information to you. Design a form in one of the pages of your Web site, and set it to send the results to your e-mail address.

It's a good idea to create all the pages for a single part of the site first, making sure to include examples of text, images, video, sound, and forms. This will become your beta test; you can test this part with the target audience before you develop the rest of the site. But before you can test it, you need to link the pages.

◎◎ Linking the Pages

Links are the lifeblood of the Web. Without links, the Internet would be simply a collection of separate, static documents. Links let site visitors move, jump, reference, search, find, move ahead, and retrace their steps. Your site design calls for many kinds of links, and it's time to implement them.

You can create links that operate with a word in the text, an icon, an image, or part of an image. You can create links to another page on your site or to another page elsewhere on the Internet. Links turn the immense compendium of items on the Internet into a usable web of connections.

Linking from Text

With a WYSIWYG web editor such as Dreamweaver, you simply select the word or phrase to be linked from and then click Make Link from the Modify menu. This opens a dialog box where you can either browse your site to find the file to link to or enter the URL of a link on another site.

A **local link**—one made to another page on your own site—might look like this in HTML:

```
<p>Please take the time to fill out our
<a href="form.html"> response form</a>.</p>
```

A link to a Web page on another site might look like this:

```
<p>You can find more information on this boat at the
<a href="http://www.tpicomp.com/pearsonyachts.html"
target="_new">TPI website</a>.</p>
```

Both approaches use the HREF attribute, which stands for "hypertext reference." The code for the local link simply states the name of the file to link to; this file is in the same folder as the file that is being linked from, so it needs no further pathname. But the link to the other site needs a full URL. It also gets a **target** parameter. The target specifies the frame or window where the page should be opened. The code shown here instructs the browser to open this site in a new browser window.

> ☆**WARNING** Opening a new window to display a linked site has a drawback. If the user forgets to close it, she will end up viewing your site in two different browser windows at once, and that might cause navigational problems.

> ☆**TIP**   Unless users specify otherwise in setting browser preferences, the linked text is displayed in blue text and underlined.

Web designers often link to other sites by opening a new window. This makes it clear to the user that this external site is not part of the sponsor's site.

To test a link, open the page in the browsers and click the link to make sure it works.

Linking from Images

Many Web pages display small images, sometimes called **icons** or **thumbnails**, that link to another page on the Web when clicked. Setting up a link from an image is exactly like setting one up from text. In Dreamweaver, you select the image, click Make Link from the Modify menu, and enter the target file or URL. Here's the HTML:

```
<a href="website/sample.html">
<img src="/images/boat.jpg"></a>
```

Note that the HREF attribute and the IMG SRC tag lie within the `<a>` and `</a>` tags.

Using Image Maps

Some images contain several different links. In the map in Figure 7.10, users can click in various places to link to various programs located across the United States.

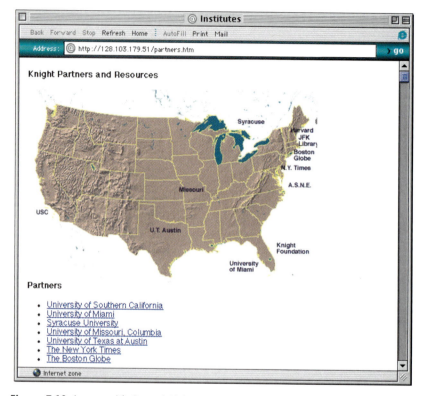

Figure 7.10 Image with Several Links

This image contains 11 hot spots that link users to 11 different Web pages. If users click Texas, they are linked to the Web page of the University of Texas at Austin. If they click New York or the word *Syracuse*, they are linked to the Orangemen's page. Users see the hot spots only when they roll over them with the mouse, at which time the pointer changes from an arrow to a hand.

These hot spots are created through an *image map*—HTML code that lists the coordinates of each hot spot along with its link URL. To design an image map, you usually use an editor (such as Dreamweaver) that contains a tool to draw the hot spots right on the image and specify the appropriate links.

To make an image map, you select the image, choose a shape from the Map tools in the Properties window, draw the hot spot on the image, and type the link URL in the box. Then you test the image map by opening the page in a Web browser and making sure all the links lead to the proper places.

The HTML code for this image map looks like this:

```
<MAP NAME=map1>
<AREA SHAPE=rect COORDS="0,150,73,208"
   HREF="partnerusc.htm">
<AREA SHAPE=rect COORDS="165,164,246,262"
   HREF="partnertexas.htm">
<AREA SHAPE=rect COORDS="214,122,283,167"
   HREF="partnermissouri.htm">
<AREA SHAPE=rect COORDS="301,242,371,268"
   HREF="partneruom.htm">
<AREA SHAPE=rect COORDS="368,213,431,242"
   HREF="partnerknight.htm">
<AREA SHAPE=rect COORDS="368,119,434,145"
   HREF="partnereditors.htm">
<AREA SHAPE=rect COORDS="375,102,434,120"
   HREF="partnertimes.htm">
<AREA SHAPE=rect COORDS="387,82,434,102"
   HREF="partnerglobe.htm">
<AREA SHAPE=rect COORDS="395,61,434,81"
   HREF="partnerjfk.htm">
<AREA SHAPE=rect COORDS="383,41,434,61"
   HREF="partnerharvard.htm">
<AREA SHAPE=rect COORDS="313,35,382,86"
   HREF="partnersyr.htm">
</MAP><IMG USEMAP="#map1" SRC="usmaplabeled.jpg">
```

All the hot spots here are rectangular, so all of them show an area shape of RECT. The coordinates indicate the horizontal and vertical locations of the upper-left and lower-right corners of each hot spot. Locations are measured in pixels from the upper-left corner of the image, which is represented as 0,0.

☆ **DO IT YOURSELF**   **Link the Pages**

Create links between the pages of your site and to pages on other sites. Link from text, link from images, and create image maps as necessary. Test these links with a Web browser.

◎◎ Dinner's Ready

If you've been cooking your Web site according to the instructions in this chapter, it should be ready for tasting. The elements have been combined in the Dreamweaver skillet, cooked in the HTML oven, and saved in their folders ready to be eaten. You may not have built every one of your site's pages, but you should have enough of them ready at this point to serve them to the target audience. In Chapter Eight you will learn how to test the site and how to publish it to a Web server.

⭐ Summary

▶ The first step in assembling pages is to create the background with an eye toward creating a pleasing color, texture, or image that's appropriate to your site's purposes.

▶ Tables are often used to arrange the various elements on the page.

▶ Using a WYSIWYG editor, it's easy to type or paste text into a Web page and place it as desired.

▶ You can control the placement and alignment of images by using a page-editing program or HTML code.

▶ You can embed sound and video files in the page (so that they run automatically), or you can display a controller that allows users to play them.

▶ You can create forms that collect feedback from users and direct it to a database or an e-mail address.

▶ After they're assembled, pages are linked to each other and to other sites on the Internet. Users can activate links by clicking on words, images, or parts of images.

⭐ Online References

ZDNet Developer. A site full of articles, ideas, and tools for the Web developer.
http://www.zdnet.com/devhead/filters/homepage/

CNET Builder.com. Excellent reviews and comparisons of various Web-authoring tools.
http://builder.cnet.com/webbuilding/0-3880.html?tag=sb

Dreamweaver information. Ideas and specifications on this WYSIWYG Web-authoring program from its publisher.
http://www.macromedia.com/software/dreamweaver/

Build a Web page with Microsoft Word. Tips and instructions from the publisher of this ubiquitous word-processing program.

Windows users visit
http://www.microsoft.com/office/word/websave.htm.

Macintosh users visit
http://www.microsoft.com/mac/products/office/2001/articles/
articles_wd.asp?Language=EN&ID=109&Page=1&Ar=Word2001

⭐ Review Questions

1. Explain the role of the background on a Web page.
2. How can text be formatted to produce a line width that's conducive to easy reading?
3. How can images be aligned with text on a Web page?
4. What parameters can you specify when embedding video on a Web page?
5. Name at least four form objects that can be used to gather data.
6. Trace the process of creating an image map in a WYSIWYG editor.

⭐ Hands-On Exercises

1. Add a background color to one of the pages you built in Chapter 6. Then add a background image to another page. Open each with a Web browser and observe the differences.
2. Embed a sound or video in your Web page so that the user can control it.
3. Create links between the pages in your site and to other Web sites.
4. Create a form that collects a name, address, and e-mail address from a user and sends it to you via e-mail. Open this page, and test the form by filling it out and submitting it. Check your e-mail to view the results.

CHAPTER EIGHT

TESTING AND POSTING THE SITE

T his chapter explains how to test your Web site from the perspectives of different types of viewers, using different Web browsers on multiple platforms over varied bandwidth and display settings. It also shows you how to publish your site on a server, whether for intranet or Internet accessibility. It explains how a Web server works and how to place the site elements on the server.

◎◎ Chapter Objectives

⭐ Learn how to test the site for five kinds of technical problems and solve the resulting design issues

⭐ Understand how to conduct productive tests with users of your site to identify and solve usability problems

⭐ Learn how to publish a site on a Web server

⭐ Learn how to register a domain name for your site and make it available to users

⭐ Understand the importance of updating your site

◉◉ Technical Testing

To accomplish its objectives, your Web site must work well on various kinds of computers in many different situations. You must ensure that the site works on the Web browsers used by your target audience and on the Windows, Macintosh, and perhaps Unix computers that these people have on their desks or laps. You must also test the site on computers with varying display (monitor) sizes and window configurations. Along the way, you must test to see how the site performs for users connected to the Internet at various bandwidths. And if the site relies on plug-ins for audio, video, animation, or interactivity, you must also test that.

Testing Browsers

What kind of browsers will your audience be using to view your site? In most cases, you can't control which browser they use, and so you must ensure that your site works on at least the two most popular browsers: Netscape Navigator and Internet Explorer. As this book is being written, about two-thirds of the Internet-using public uses Explorer, and most of the others use Netscape. Other browsers make up about 2% of the total. But these statistics may not match your audience. For example, if your site is for a company intranet and your company has standardized on Netscape, you need not test with Explorer. But most Web designers need to make sure the site works acceptably on both popular browsers.

A **browser** receives the HTML code from a Web page, interprets it, and displays its interpretation of the code's instructions in the window. Because Explorer and Netscape interpret things a little differently, your pages will seldom be displayed identically on each browser. And because users set their own preferences for the display of text and certain other features, you cannot guarantee that all your users will see the same thing. Figures 8.1 and 8.2 show the same Web page displayed in the two browsers. Can you see the differences?

In this example, the paragraph of text displays in a different size and font; the frames are drawn differently; and the images line up differently.

To test your site, it need not be posted to the server. You can test it from your local disk. First, make sure that both Netscape and Explorer are installed on your computer. Open Explorer, and click Open File under the File menu, and open your home page. Then restore the Explorer window to a size of about 800 by 600 pixels. Next, open Netscape, click Open under the File menu, and then click Page in Navigator, and open your home page again. Restore the Netscape window to the same size as the Explorer window. With the same page open in both browsers and with the windows open to the same size, switch back and forth to look for differences.

Figure 8.1 Web Page Displayed in Internet Explorer

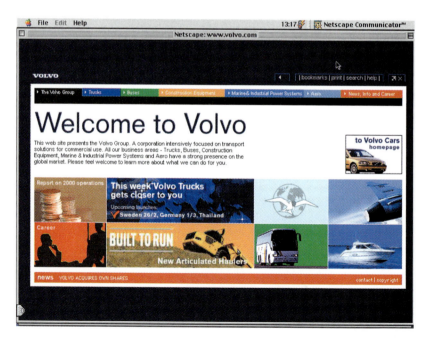

Figure 8.2 Web Page Displayed in Netscape

Differences alone should not cause you to revise the Web page. The question to ask is whether the design is executed successfully in both browsers. The display need not be identical, but it needs to work for the user in both Netscape and Explorer.

What issues should you look for? Here are some key concerns:

⭐ The way text is displayed

⭐ The way images align with each other and with the text

⭐ The ways that tables are arranged

⭐ The ways that sound, video, and animations are handled

If these differ slightly between platforms but do not alter the user experience, you can safely ignore the differences. But if your site works well in one browser but not the other, you should make changes so that the page displays acceptably in both browsers.

While you have the pages open in the browsers, check to see what the text looks like at various font sizes. In both Netscape and Explorer, users can set their own preferences for font display size, and many people do. You must be sure that your pages work at various font size preferences. Figures 8.3 and 8.4 show an example.

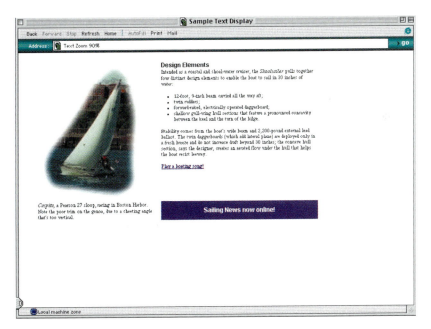

Figure 8.3 Page Shown at 90% Text Zoom

Figure 8.4 Page Shown at 120% Text Zoom

The page looks different in both instances, but it works the same, and no design elements have been compromised. Both users would achieve the same result from this page.

Testing Platforms

What kinds of computers do your site visitors use? Are your audience members accountants, using run-of-the-mill Windows 98 desktops? Or are they graphic artists working on Macintosh G4s loaded with memory-intensive applications? Or are they senior citizens surfing the Internet at home using inexpensive Dells or iMacs? Perhaps they are salespeople on the road using lightweight laptops running Windows 2000, or college students using iBooks. Chances are, your audience includes some people in each group. So you will need to make sure your site works on these different platforms.

A **platform** consists of a combination of hardware and software: a computer plus its operating system. Examples are a Gateway desktop running Windows 98, a Macintosh G3 running OS9, an IBM ThinkPad running Windows 2000, and so forth. You can't test the site on every possible platform, but you must test on those platforms typically used by your target audience.

As this book is written, about 90% of Web browsers are using the Windows platform. Another 10% are using Macintosh, and a few are using Unix or Linux. For most sites, testing with Windows and Macintosh is sufficient.

> ⭐ **TIP**   **Internet Everywhere?**
>
> Futurists predict that the Internet will soon move beyond personal computers to connect all kinds of devices, from home furnaces to cell phones to Palm Pilots to automobiles. This means that future Web designers may need to test pages in an array of settings not antici-pated in this book. This evolution will engender new possibilities in HTML and JavaScript and will require new kinds of WYSIWYG editors and browsers. Designers may need to build several versions of the same site: a text-only version for mobilephone users, a pic-tures-only version for Web TV viewers, and an abbreviated version for browsing on a Handspring Visor.

The most practical way to test different platforms is to set up a Windows system like the one most likely to be used by a typical target visitor along with a similar Macintosh system, and then see how the pages work on both. If you haven't yet posted the site to a server, you will have to place a copy of the site on a storage medium that can be read by both Macintosh and Windows platforms. Here are some approaches:

⭐ Local area network (LAN): If your organization supports a LAN, copy the site (all folders) to a volume on the LAN that can be seen from both Macintosh and Windows computers on the network. To test the site, log on to the shared volume and then open the Web page file from the browser. Use Open File and not Open Location.

⭐ CD-ROM: Copy the Web site onto a hybrid CD-ROM—one that can be read by both Macintosh and Windows. Then insert the CD-ROM in each comput-er in turn and test the operation of the site.

⭐ Zip or floppy disk: Because Macintosh computers can read Windows-format-ted floppy and zip disks, you can copy the contents of your site onto such a disk and move it back and forth between the two computers to test it.

Again, the goal is not identical appearance but acceptable performance. If the column of text on your page averages 9 words per line on Macintosh and 11 words on Windows, you need not make any change. But if half your page disappears because the framesets work differently on the two platforms, you'll need to redesign the page.

The most noticeable differences between the two platforms relate to fonts and colors. The two operating systems use different fonts and display them on the screen in different sizes. In addition, the colors on Windows tend to display dark-er than the colors on Macintosh. Certain plug-ins work slightly differently on the two platforms, so you must carefully test all audio, video, and animation. A later section ("Testing Plug-Ins") describes how to test these plug-in media files.

You may also uncover filename problems, especially if you authored your site on Macintosh and are testing it for the first time on Windows. The Macintosh operating system is quite forgiving when it comes to filenames and often lets you get away with illegal filenames, such as those containing spaces or lacking the proper extension. A site containing such errors may work well on Macintosh. But the first test on Windows will result in many "file not found" errors and blank spaces where images should appear. If you experience these problems, check all filenames for proper form: no spaces, correct file extensions, no special characters.

To be thorough, you should test both browsers on both platforms because Netscape and Explorer interpret things slightly differently on Windows than on Macintosh. In the Multimedia Development Lab at the Boston University College of Communication, for instance, testers set up four computers in a row to test student projects:

★ A Windows computer running Netscape

★ A Windows computer running Explorer

★ A Macintosh running Netscape

★ A Macintosh running Explorer

This setup makes it easy to spot problems and makes testing more efficient.

Testing Displays

Many Web designers enjoy large, high-resolution monitors and fast video display circuitry on their desktop computers. But most members of the target audience may be using low-end, low-resolution displays that take forever to draw a JPEG image on the screen. Many users have set their displays to 640 by 480 pixels and do not know how to change them. Others have lowered the color depth to a setting that makes a beautiful sunset photo look like a mud puddle. For these reasons, you must test the site under varying display conditions.

Pixel Setting

The most common display setting for computers is 800 by 600 pixels, but this is far from universal. Some users may own computers capable of a larger size but have their monitors set to a lower resolution. Others may be using an old computer that's restricted to a 640 by 480-pixel display. Users of high-end computers may enjoy resolutions of 1024 by 768 pixels and beyond. The easiest way to see what your site will look like at these resolutions is to find a computer capable of resizing itself to the three most common resolutions and view your site at all three.

To change the resolution of your display in Windows, click Settings from the Start menu. Then click Control Panel, and then double-click Display. In the Display Properties dialog box, click the Settings tab. Move the slider to the desired resolution, click OK, and wait a moment while the display resets itself. Then open a browser, and from there open your site. View several pages, and take notes on any problems that arise. Use this method to try all three resolutions: 640 × 480, 800 × 600, and 1024 × 768.

To change resolution on Macintosh, use the control tab that looks like a monitor with dots. Click and hold, and then slide up to the resolution you want to try.

Consider the results of this test with an eye to the most likely display resolution used by your target audience. Most Web designers aim at the 800 by 600-pixel display. This means that viewers who use a smaller resolution must scroll the page, and larger displays gain some extra space. You can't accommodate every variation; the important consideration is to understand the way the site will look to various users.

Color Depth

Most computer users work with their monitors set to a 16-bit color depth (thousands of colors), but others have switched down to an 8-bit color depth (256 colors). A few power users employ 24-bit color (millions of colors). Most people can't see the difference between 16- and 24-bit color, so testing at 16- and 8-bit color depths should suffice for most Web sites. The differences in color depth will be most evident in JPEG photos and videos.

It's easiest to test the site for color depth while you're testing the resolution because the methods for switching are similar. To change the resolution of your display in Windows, click Settings from the Start menu, and then click Control Panel and double-click Display. In the Display Properties dialog box, click the Settings tab. Here, choose a color depth from the drop-down Colors menu list on the left. Click OK, and wait a moment while the display resets itself. Then open a browser, and from there open your site. View several pages, and take notes on any problems that arise. Use this method to try at least 8-bit and 16-bit color.

To change color depth on Macintosh, use the control tab that looks like a monitor with colored stripes. Click and hold, and then slide up to the color depth you want to try.

Testing Bandwidths

Sites with large photos, sound, and video are affected more by differences in bandwidth than by any other factor. The differences in users' connection speeds are far greater than those in browsers, resolution, or color depth. Some of your visitors may be receiving data at 1,000,000 bytes per second, whereas others are getting only 5000. For users having fast connections, your full-screen photo of the company CEO will appear in less than a second. Other users will wait several minutes for the picture to download. Testing the site under the same conditions experienced by your audience will help you understand the effectiveness of the site.

The only way to test the various bandwidths is to put the site on a Web server, set up a computer under various connection methods, and try it out. The next section explains how to post your site to a Web server. Table 8.1 shows the kind of performance you might expect from various connection methods.

Few institutions or organizations maintain all five connection methods in a single building, so this test may be the most difficult. But the chief limitations for users will show up at the 56K modem speed, which is easy to set up using a computer with a modem. It's important for you personally to experience what it's like to view your site at the slowest bandwidth. Viewing many graphics-intensive sites is almost impossible when each image takes almost 10 seconds to load under optimum conditions. If your site uses images for menus and navigation, users must wait for all images to load before making any choices or seeing any content.

Table 8.1 Performance of Various Connection Methods

Connection Method	Estimated Bandwidth	Seconds to Download a 50K File
56K modem	56K	7.1
ISDN line	128K	3.1
DSL	128–512K	1.6
Cable modem	512K	0.8
LAN	1MB+	0.4

> ☆ **WARNING** **The World Wide Wait**
>
> How long will your audience be willing to wait before viewing an image or watching a video on your site? Some observers note that typical web users have a limit of about eight seconds, after which they move on to another page. Careful testing with your target audience will help you determine their limit, and revise your pages accordingly.

If your bandwidth testing shows usability problems for modem users, consider making these changes to the site to reduce download time and increase usability:

☆ Use fewer images. Images are the culprit in most low-bandwidth situations. A single 320 by 240-pixel mage can require 50K of data, taking almost 10 seconds of download time on a modem. An entire page of text, in contrast, needs only 1K and will download in less than a second. A page with four quarter-page images could take more than 40 seconds, and few people will wait this long. If this is a problem, consider using fewer images and more text.

☆ Compress the images. If your site's objectives call for certain images, make sure they are compressed as much as possible. To do this, open each of your JPEG images in Photoshop. Click Save As from the File menu, and then choose a higher compression ratio. Compression will lower the image's visual quality somewhat, but it can reduce the file size to a comfortable download time.

☆ Use text for navigation. Research for this book revealed several sites that used pictures, rather than text, for navigation buttons. One site ran a menu bar across the bottom of the screen, as shown in Figure 8.5.

BMW Group sites | BMW in your country | Careers | News | Dialogue | Site map | Help | Language | Copyright

Figure 8.5 Menu Bar Composed of Images

Each item in this menu bar was created as a GIF image about 20K in size. So users must download a 180K menu bar before they can see or use it. That takes 30 or 40 seconds. (If the user rolls over one of the images, downloading takes even longer because each image is scripted with JavaScript to show an alternative image on rollover.) The designer could have created a similar menu bar for a fraction of the download time by using a table and text, as shown in Figure 8.6.

Group sites   In your country   Careers   News   Dialogue   Site map   Help   Language   Copyright

Figure 8.6 Menu Bar Made with Text in a Table

This menu bar occupies only 1.5K and so will download to the modem user in less than a second. It may not be as pretty, but it works exactly the same as the image-based menu bar that takes 30 times longer to download. It also took considerably less time to build.

So unplug your LAN connection or cable modem, plug in the telephone line, and try viewing your site at low bandwidth. You may be surprised by what you see, and you may be led to make changes that will improve your site's functionality. Like the cook who steps out of the kitchen and into the dining room every once in a while to see how the diners are doing, you should view your work from the perspective of the customer. Your culinary creation may look and smell delicious on the stove, but it may lose something on the way to the dinner table. Only by sitting at the table and tasting your own dishes will you understand the dining experience and learn how to make it better.

Testing Plug-Ins

While testing your site on various platforms and browsers, you will confront plug-in problems if the site uses audio, video, or Flash animations. Some computers won't have the needed plug-in installed. Some browsers will have configured the plug-in in a way that will thwart the display of your multimedia file. Others will lack a codec or system extension necessary to decompress your site's elements.

A complete explanation of plug-ins for multimedia is included in Addison-Wesley's *The Web Wizard's Guide to Multimedia*. Meanwhile, here's an overview. From your testing experience, you will learn the information users need to get the right plug-ins and to configure them properly so that they can work with your site. At a minimum, you need to provide users with the following information:

⭐ Which plug-ins, if any, are needed to view the elements of your site

⭐ Where to download the plug-ins

⭐ How to install each plug-in

⭐ How to configure the plug-in in the browser to fit the needs of your site

After testing, you may need to add some instructions and warnings about the plug-ins. You may also discover that some of your multimedia elements simply won't work on certain combinations of browser and platform, no matter how the plug-in is configured. In this case, you must either find another way to display the information or provide a warning on the page.

> ☆ **DO IT YOURSELF**   **Test the Site**
>
> Test your Web site for technical problems according to the suggestions in this chapter. Make a note of any problem areas, and then fix any sections that do not work correctly under all circumstances. Then test again, and repeat this process until you arrive at an acceptable site.

◎◎ User Testing

So far, you've conducted only technical tests. But the true test of a site is in the hands and minds of the target audience. The diligent Web designer will find opportunities to put the site in front of typical users and collect reactions from them. Better yet, you'll watch over the shoulders of some of your users and observe how they approach the site and navigate through it.

Through this process of user testing, you will learn several things:

☆ People come to your site for different reasons, and this affects the way they use it. Some are casual browsers, stumbling upon your page in search of other things, and will not notice minor problems. Others are driven and committed to get the information they need for their own pressing projects, and these visitors will notice every detail of functionality. Still others are loyal customers, members of your organization's community, who will want the site to serve their purposes exactly and may suggest a hundred ideas for improvement.

☆ Different computing situations result in very different user experiences. You should conduct user testing under the varied conditions you expect of your audience: different browsers, different platforms, and different connection speeds. Such testing will expose problems not uncovered even in the most careful technical tests.

☆ Some users need more help than others. Some of them may breeze right through the site and find what they need without any problems or confusion. Others may find themselves stuck, not sure of where to go next or how to find help. Some visitors are Web aficionados, well versed in the arcane crafts of plug-in installation and streaming media, but others have learned only how to point and click. Watching target users at work on your site will help you redesign the site to better serve their needs.

Collecting User Reactions

A number of options are available for collecting user feedback to your site. If you're observing users at work, it's important to make notes. Another approach is to ask for their feedback directly. To do that, ask them to complete a questionnaire or checklist. Or ask them to talk aloud as they browse your site, describing what they are doing and thinking, and record what they say. For unattended feedback, add an online user questionnaire with the results sent back to you in an e-mail.

After you've gathered user reactions, think them over and then make a list of the things that need to be changed. Then go back and modify the pages that need improvement.

⭐ **DO IT YOURSELF   User Testing**

Conduct user testing of your site. Find some people like those in your target audience, sit them down at a computer typical of the type used by your site visitors, and watch them as they work. Make note of what they do (or don't do). Talk with them about their experience. Gather their suggestions for improving the site. Then revise your work based on the results of this test.

It's time to post the revised and improved version of the site to its permanent home on the Web server. That's the subject of the next section.

◎◎ Posting the Site

The audience for your site will not be able to see it over the Internet until it is posted to a Web server. This section explains how Web servers work and how to post your site to the server.

Types of Web Servers

If you've built your site following the guidelines set forth in this book, it should run on almost any kind of Web server. A **Web server** is simply a computer connected to the Internet and running software that serves up Web files. Any computer can be a Web server, but in most instances your site will be posted to a computer specially designed and situated to act only as a Web server. These servers are kept running 24 hours a day, are carefully maintained, and are used only for serving files to Internet users.

As this book is being written, the most popular large-scale Web servers are as follows:

⭐ Unix: Unix computers run Unix, a fast, reliable, industrial-strength operating system. They are manufactured by IBM, Sun, Hewlett-Packard, and other companies. In the beginning, all Web servers were Unix computers. In the Unix environment, a Web-serving application, such as Apache, actually serves the HTML files in response to user requests.

⭐ Windows NT: Microsoft's NT/2000 Server operating system running on a high-capacity computer with Intel's chipset is often used as a Web server in organizations whose LANs are served through Windows NT. The NT Server software includes an Internet Information Server (IIS) application that serves the Web files to Internet users.

⭐ Mac OSX: These high-speed computers, manufactured by Apple, are used extensively for video streaming as well as Web serving. They run a special version of the Unix operating system and often use Apache as an HTTP server.

How Servers Work

Here's an example of how a server works:

1. A user clicks a button on a Web page that links to a page showing the design of a new sailboat.

2. The user's Web browser sends a message to the server's **Internet Protocol** (IP) address. The message reads something like, "Computer number 128.197.193.232, please send me, computer number 192.168.1.1, the file `design.htm`."

3. This message travels through cyberspace looking for the computer it's directed at. Routers along the way look at the IP address (the number) on the message and send it in that direction.

4. The server (IP number 128.197.193.232) receives the message and sends the file `design.htm` to computer number 192.168.1.1.

5. The user's computer receives the `design.htm` file, where it is interpreted by the Web browser and displayed on the screen.

> ☆ **TIP**   **IP Addresses and Domain Name Servers**
>
> Each computer on the Internet is assigned its own unique IP address. The numbers are assigned by the user's Internet service provider, which in turn gets its list of IP numbers from the international Internet committee. Computers can also be given **domain names**, such as `www.nytimes.com` or `mmcom.bu.edu`, which are easier for users to remember. The names are matched with the numbers in a database. When you send a request to `mmcom.bu.edu`, the request goes to a **domain name server**, which looks it up in the database and sends it to 128.197.192.1.

Posting the Files

No matter what platform or software your server uses, you must post the files to the server. There are three ways to do this:

☆ On disk or CD-ROM: You copy the entire site to a floppy, zip, or CD-ROM and take it to the company Web master (the person who holds the keys to the Web server). Then you watch as the Web master inserts the medium and copies the files to the appropriate directory on the Web server.

☆ Through the local area network: You connect to the Web server through the LAN and copy the site files to the appropriate directory. This method usually requires a password from the Web master.

☆ Over the Internet: You use **File Transfer Protocol** (FTP) to log on to the Web server (from anywhere in the world), locate the appropriate directory, and use FTP to transfer the Web site files to the server. This method also requires a password from the Web master.

In most cases, the person in charge of the Web server will have set up a directory for your site. She will also assign you a user name and password that will allow you to copy files to that directory. No matter which method of posting you use, you must copy all the files and folders from your Web site folder to the directory on the Web server. The files and folders must be organized on the Web server just as they are in your site folder. In other words, the directory structure must remain intact.

⭐ **SHORTCUT**   To help with posting the site, you can use software such as Web Publishing Wizard for Windows or Fetch for Macintosh. These programs set up a connection to the Web server, send the user name and password, and allow easy copying of the files. Many WYSIWYG Web editors include this capability in their site management tools. Some can be set to save files automatically to the Web server whenever they are saved to the designer's computer.

⭐ **DO IT YOURSELF**   **Post the Site**

Use one of the methods described in this chapter to post your site to a Web server. Then test it with a browser to ensure its proper operation.

The site is posted and ready for the audience to browse. But how will users know where to connect?

◉◉ Making the Connection

Each Web server has a unique domain name. The XYZ Corporation might name its server (with the permission of the domain names authority) `www.xyz.com`. On that server, the Web master might set up a directory for your Web site called `boatdesigns`. To connect to your site, users simply type `http://www.xyz.com/boatdesigns` into the browser.

⭐ **WARNING**   For this to work smoothly, you should name the home page of the site `index.html` or `default.html`. Many Web servers automatically send the page having that name to any user who sends a request to the directory. The organization's Web master can tell you which filename to use.

But suppose that some people in your target audience don't know your domain name or even that your site exists. How will they find you? This is where **search engines** and **directories** come into play. Some search engines automatically browse the Internet, looking for new sites and adding them to their index. Others must be told that your site exists before it shows up in their directory. A wise Web designer will contact the major search engines and directories and take steps to get the new site listed.

⭐ **TIP**   **Domain Names**

To register a domain name in the DNS database, you need the permission of private organizations designated by the international Internet committee, such as Network Solutions, Inc. For a nominal fee (usually less than $100), your domain name is added as long as it isn't already registered to someone else. For a fee, many Internet service providers will manage your application and provide you with space on their Web server, something called **Web site hosting**.

Each search engine provides online instructions for doing this on its home page. Your target users are much more likely to find your site if it is listed in the most popular search engines and directories, such as Yahoo, AltaVista, Google, and Lycos.

Keeping It Fresh

Your work is not finished when the site is posted. It may never be finished. A good Web site offers something new to its users every time they connect. It modifies its files based on user feedback. It finds and deploys new technologies that help its users accomplish their objectives faster and easier. You must keep track of the site's progress by tracking its traffic, querying its users, and measuring the accomplishment of its objectives.

The successful master chef reads the reviews of the restaurant, is always on the lookout for new ways of cooking, and is not afraid to experiment with new dishes. In the same way, the Web designer should periodically revisit the design process from the beginning and strive to better serve the site's audience.

⭐ Summary

▶ To make sure your site can be viewed effectively by the target audience, you must test it on at least two kinds of browsers (Netscape and Explorer), on various computing platforms (especially Windows and Macintosh), at various display settings for screen size and color depth, and using various connection methods and bandwidths.

▶ You may need to adapt the site design in response to issues that arise when you test the site with target users in typical situations.

▶ The method for posting the site to the server depends on the type of server used by the organization and the Web master's policies for access.

▶ After your site is posted, you should keep it fresh by updating the contents, responding to user feedback, and upgrading it technologically.

⭐ Online References

User-Testing Techniques: Site Reviews. From the All Things Web site, a useful explication of the process of testing a site.
http://www.pantos.org/atw/35283.html

User testing. A collection of how-to articles from Builder.com on how to plan and conduct a formal test of your site.
http://www.builder.com/Graphics/Evaluation/

Why You Need to Test Your Web Site with Real Users. Some friendly answers to this question from Webreference.
http://www.webreference.com/authoring/design/usability/testing/

Cyberatlas Statistics Toolbox. A regularly updated directory of sources for statistics on which browser, which server, and which platforms people are using.
http://cyberatlas.internet.com/big_picture/stats_toolbox/article

⭐ Review Questions

1. Explain why a site must be tested on both Netscape and Explorer.
2. List at least two user preference settings that can affect the way a Web page displays.

3. Trace the process of conducting a technical test of a Web site.

4. Explain the effect of display size and color depth on the functionality of a Web page.

5. List some of the ways to improve a site's performance for users who have low-bandwidth connections.

6. Name at least three reasons to test a Web site with actual users from the target audience.

7. Describe two Web server platforms.

8. Explain how a Web server accomplishes its tasks.

9. Trace the process of posting a Web site to a server.

☆ Hands-On Exercises

1. View a multimedia Web site first with Netscape and then with Explorer. Observe the differences, if any, in display and functionality.

2. Develop a small Web site, and test it on both platforms and both browsers. Make a note of any differences you observe in the four situations.

3. Connect to a corporate Web site, and view it at three different display sizes and color depths. Notice any differences in functionality.

4. Connect to a corporate Web site from an office or lab with high-speed Internet access. Then go home and connect from a modem. Observe and report the differences in performance.

5. Make a list of what you would change on the site you viewed in Exercise 4, and explain how you would make the modification.

6. Develop a small Web site having some dead-ends and poorly designed pages. Test it with some naïve users, and collect their comments and reactions.

7. Work with the Web master in your organization to post one of the small sites you developed to the Web server. Connect to this site through the Internet.

APPENDIX: ANSWERS TO ODD-NUMBERED REVIEW QUESTIONS

Chapter One

1. Define the audience; state the purpose; define the functions; design the structure; determine the best media.

3. A site that is built around the perceptions and vocabulary of the sponsoring company would be organization-centric. A site that focuses on a certain set of software or design tools would be technology-centered. A site built around the perceptions, vocabulary, and needs of its audience is considered user-centered. User-centered design is what we're after.

5. Choose, animate, search and find, buy and sell, manipulate, construct, question and answer, converse, play.

7. Compressed music files, with samples of the songs on the CDs, would be important, compressed so much that they need little bandwidth, since people who live in rural areas (out in the country) are less likely to enjoy high-speed Internet connections than people who live in cities. Images of country music artists, and text about the songs and the singers, would also be important. So might interactive forums and chats and databases where fans could share information about the stars.

Chapter Two

1. Magazines are taller than they are wide, while web pages are the opposite. Magazines enjoy much higher resolution than a Web page. Magazines can be presented in smaller (8 or 9 point) type than is possible with a Web page. Magazines do not need to include navigation tools and information on every page, as Web pages do. Web pages can include hypertext links, video, and sound, while magazines printed on paper cannot.

3. You might use a table to display a comparative list of items and attributes on a Web page. A table can also serve as a grid on which to display images in an orderly arrangement of rows and columns. A table can form the columns in a newspaper or magazine-like display of text and images on a Web page. A table is a good way to display numerical data and measurements along multiple variables.

5. A horizontal menu can appear across the top or bottom of a Web page. A vertical menu can be listed down one side. A menu can pop up when the user presses the mouse on it. A menu can be made of thumbnail images.

7. The organization can display its corporate colors in the design of the site. It can include the company logo on each page. It can use the same font as its print publications. It can incorporate design features such as shapes and special visual effects that are used in its products and in its advertising.

◎◎ Chapter Three

1. Many print publications, such as magazines, are taller than they are wide. But the computer screen is wider than it is tall. Designs based on tall aspect publications do not work well on a computer screen. A designer must consider the display size of the computers used by typical members of the audience that will view the site, ensuring that they will be able to see the entire width of the Web page without scrolling.

3. The designer must consider the organization's corporate color scheme, the warm and cold nature of various colors, the ways that colors in combination can create contrast or complementarity, and the ease of reading text on a colored background.

5. The sketch allows the Web designer to visualize the overall layout of the page, encourages the consideration of alternatives, enables a precise pixel-by-pixel measurement of the various elements to be displayed, and permits the designer to get feedback on the design from various reviewers.

7. Web designers use pencil and paper, Photoshop, Word, and WYSIWYG Web-page editors to sketch and prototype their sites.

◎◎ Chapter Four

1. If you count each image, background, menu item, column of text, and navigation button, many Web sites include several dozen separate elements.

3. You enter the labels and values into the cells of the spreadsheet, then enter any formulas that will help analyze and aggregate the data. By selecting rows and columns of the spreadsheet, then creating a chart, you can make a graphic image of the data. The chart can be saved as a GIF file, and the table of data can be saved as a text file for later importation into the Web page.

5. You open the photograph in an image-editing program such as Photoshop. Then you set the resolution and size of the image to fit the specification of your page design. Next you modify the image by cropping, brightening, shading, and editing. When it's complete, you save it in a format suitable for inclusion in a Web page.

7. Marquee, Move, Pencil, Line, Zoom, Smudge, and other tools from the tool palette; adjustments for brightness, contrast, and color and others from the Image menu; various effects from the Filter menu, such as stylize, blur, and sharpen.

Chapter Five

1. If you count each image, background, menu item, column of text, video clip, sound file, and navigation button, many Web sites include several dozen separate elements.

3. In their uncompressed form, these multimedia files contain many megabytes of information that would take much too long to travel over the Internet from the Web server to the audience. Compression reduces the file size considerably so that users will not have to wait as long to receive the information.

Chapter Six

1. Using "Save as HTML" from Word is very easy to do and can create a very simple Web page. An HTML editor is flexible and useful to someone who knows HTML code. A WYSIWYG editor allows non-programmers to create complex Web sites.

3. Each file must have it proper filename extension, such as .html for Web pages, .jpg or .gif for images, .aif for sounds, .mov for video. Files should be organized into directories for ease of access. The names of all directories and files must be suitable for Web transmission, with no spaces and no special characters.

5. A frame can be used to display a title or menu that is unchanged throughout the site, as other content is displayed in a different and changing frame. A table can be used to set up a consistent grid for the display of text or images on a series of Web pages.

◎◎ Chapter Seven

1. The background can be left blank, display a solid color or texture, or show an image. The background appears under text, images, and other elements on the page. The Web designer must be careful that the background not make the content difficult to see or read.

3. Images and text can be placed into the cells of a table so that they are aligned as the designer desires. Images can also be aligned left, right, top, or bottom in relation to the text that flows around them.

5. Form objects to gather data include fields, text areas, radio buttons, check boxes, and option menus.

◎◎ Chapter Eight

1. In most situations, the Web designer has no control over which browser the audience will use to view the site, and thus must assume that some will use Netscape and others Explorer. The site must work well in both browsers, to serve the needs of all users.

3. The site must be tested with both browsers to make sure all items display and operate to meet the needs of the audience. The site should also be tested on both Windows and Macintosh platforms with the kinds of computers likely to be used by the audience. As it is being tested, the designer should look at it under different display resolutions and color depths. The site should be viewed from the bandwidths typical of the viewing audience. Finally, any media that require plug-ins should be tested under all of the conditions described above.

5. Performance can be improved by using fewer and smaller images; by reducing the size and number of sound and video files; by compressing images to a smaller file size; and by using text rather than images for navigation.

7. A Unix Web server is a fast, industrial-strength server. A Windows NT server often performs other tasks for an organization, as well as serving Web pages. A Macintosh OSX server uses the Unix operating system. Any computer connected to the Internet can be configured as a Web server.

9. First, the Web designer must contact the Web master for the server on which the site is to be posted. In most cases, the Web master will set up a directory for the site and assign the designer a username and password. The designer then copies the files to the directory on the Web server through a LAN or via FTP.

INDEX

CREDITS

Figure 1.1	Reproduced with permission of Yahoo! Inc. © 2000 by Yahoo! Inc. YAHOO! and the YAHOO! logo are trademarks of Yahoo! Inc.
Figure 1.3	Courtesy of NOAA
Figure 1.7	Web site courtesy of J. Crew
Figure 1.18	James Lengel for the Harvard Graduate School of Education
Figure 2.1	Reprinted with the permission of the Regents of the University of Minnesota. © 2001 Regents of the University of Minnesota.
Figure 2.5	Killeen, Kieran M. and Kimura, Mark M. © 2000. Stein and Schools Lecture Series: Policy, Planning and Design for a 21st Century Public Education System. Clarence S. Stein Institute for Urban and Landscape Studies at Cornell University. Ithaca, New York.
Figure 2.6	© Lands' End, Inc. Used with permission.
Figure 2.13	General Electric Company © 1997-2001
Figure 3.4	Courtesy of Tammy Kohlleppel and Jennifer Bradley, University of Florida
Figure 4.2	© WHO
Figure 6.1	Reprinted with permission from Bare Bones Software, Inc.
Figure 6.3	BOSTON UNIVERSITY
Figure 7.1	© SJL Images/Stephen Jay Lunsford